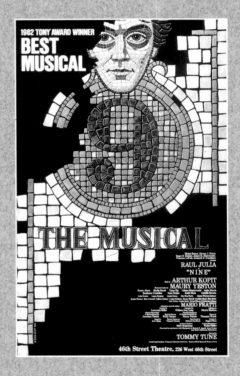

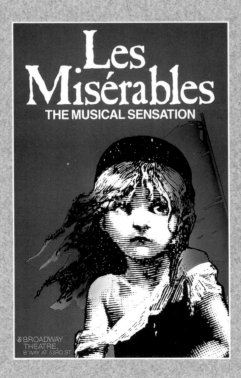

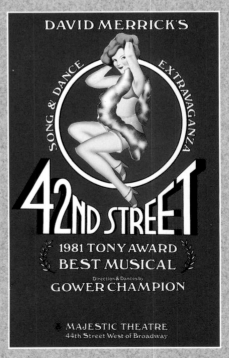

MARTIN GOTTFRIED

MORE BROADWAY MUSICALS

SINCE 1980

WITH PHOTOGRAPHS BY MARTHA SWOPE AND OTHERS

HARRY N. ABRAMS, INC., PUBLISHERS, NEW YORK

FOR MY BEAUTIFUL, BRIGHT, DARLING DAUGHTER, MAYA

Editor: Robert Morton/Designer: Warren Infield/ Photo Editor: John K. Crowley

Library of Congress Cataloging-in-Publication Data

Gottfried, Martin.
    More Broadway musicals/Martin Gottfried: with photographs by Martha Swope and others.
    p. cm.
    Includes index.
    ISBN 0-8109-3621-6
    1. Musicals—New York (N.Y.)—History and criticism. I. Title.
ML1711.8.N3G69   1991
782.1'4'097471—dc20   91-8030
                                                                    CIP
                                                                    MN

Published in 1991 by Harry N. Abrams, Incorporated, New York.
A Times Mirror Company

TABLE
OF
CONTENTS

INTRODUCTION

In the years since *Broadway Musicals* was published in 1979, it sometimes seemed as if there might be no more Broadway musicals. Some years there were so few that the annual Tony Awards had to be cut back for want of eligible shows and twice the New York drama critics found no musical worth calling a season's best. The alarm was sounded that the British were coming, or had already come with *Evita*, *Cats*, *Les Misérables* and *The Phantom of the Opera* to rechristen Broadway's baby the West End musical, and those shows seemed not only British but decidedly un-Broadway. They didn't look like *Annie Get Your Gun* or *Fiddler on the Roof* and the howl to be heard was enraged.

But along with the howl could be heard the wail of a newborn, or at least reborn Broadway baby, for over seventy new musicals came to New York between 1979 and 1991 and they ranged from nostalgic revivals, or else the traditional song and dance, to a new kind of musical that had not been seen before, which were the biggest hits of all.

Die-hard stage conservatives resisted mightily. They loved musicals so dearly that they wanted them to stay the same forever. The success of a new kind of musical seemed to mean the end of the old but change is growth, of course; life itself. And this change was evolutionary. The musical theater was merely adjusting to a contemporary sensibility. *Evita*, *Cats*, *Les Misérables* and *The Phantom of the Opera* perhaps seemed like new kinds of musicals but they were performing for audience approval in the same way as shows always did and audiences are the only judge that ever mattered in a commercial theater like Broadway's.

The entirely sung, British-made musicals were not the only ones to stand out on Broadway in these years. Stephen Sondheim, the most brilliant musical dramatist of our times, continued his pursuit of an artistic distillation of the Broadway musical spirit. Too, there were several successful musicals in the traditional mold — *42nd Street* and *La Cage aux Folles*. But who could deny that the fertile days of musical

Cats was the musical that established Andrew Lloyd Webber as the dominating composer on Broadway.

12

comedy had ended? The cost of producing a musical had so escalated that showmaking was no longer a free and easy process. Big business and a new, international market had raised the stakes and the pressure. Ticket prices rising to an undreamed of $100 made a night at the theater more than a casual entertainment event.

And yet for all that, the excitement of a George Gershwin tune or a Jule Styne overture was still recognizable as the house lights dimmed at the tingling start of a *Phantom of the Opera* or a *Grand Hotel*. The anticipation of a Broadway musical about to start was still enough to stir the imagination and set the heart racing.

Throughout this elongated decade of change and stress, from the end of the 1970s into the start of the 1990s, Broadway was defined and comforted by the enduring presence of *A Chorus Line*, the artistic musical about commercial musicals and a reminder of the roots of musical theater. It would be fifteen years before this archetypical show closed on April 28, 1990 after 6,137 performances; as definitively as it concluded an era, so it began a new one. For *A Chorus Line* paid homage to conventional musical comedy using the techniques of *concept musicals* — a ballet-like collage of book, music, lyric and dance. Moreover, as its ghostly dancers high-kicked into the fading lights, the music of Andrew Lloyd Webber could be heard in rising underscore. The British composer with his singular combination of show tunes, operatic technique and stage sense was almost single-handedly revitalizing Broadway musicals. Whatever could be said about him (and he seemed to be the only subject of theatrical conversation for the entire decade) his shows were *popular* and it was a popularity that had fertilized our musicals from the start. Popularity had swept them past the scorn of intellectuals and now an invigorated audience swept past a similarly humorless scorn to return and reflect the energy radiating from the stages. In a time when Broadway's professional musical makers were losing touch with audiences, Webber's shows became the backbone of a renewed Broadway. Indeed, musicals became virtually the only kind of theater there *was* on Broadway.

No matter how sophisticated musicals may become, they always will be defined at the box office and measured by audience passion. More than any other kind of theater, musicals are children of Broadway, the most commercial of all stages, and they will always draw their energy from the need to satisfy a paying theatergoer.

A flop fails to fulfill this transaction. It does not deliver on the advertised tears and thrills. But when a show does come through on this ticket exchange, the box office attraction is irresistible. The audience rushes shamelessly to the darkened hall and the brilliant haven of the shining proscenium. That is the heady atmosphere around a hit Broadway musical.

For a long time this atmosphere was associated exclusively with standard model shows — musicals with show business pizzazz. It was as if a Broadway musical had to be *a Broadway musical*. Overtures and walk-out music were the norm, necessary to send audiences home whistling "Shall We Dance?" Any variation on the formula constituted a disappointment, if not an outright offense.

And then *A Chorus Line* opened in 1975, saying just about all that could be said in summation of that genre and, in fact, of an era. It was time for a new book to begin.

Perhaps not everything about *A Chorus Line* was perfect, but certainly everything done afterward would be compared to it in spirit, and as the theater moved into

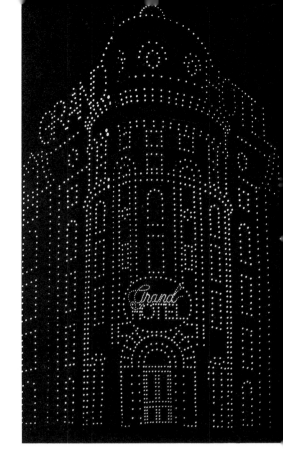

For *Grand Hotel*, director Tommy Tune reversed the traditional sequence of a Broadway musical by opening the show with curtain calls and closing it with this front curtain designed by Tony Walton. Picture curtains, once seen at the start of every musical, have all but disappeared.

Overleaf:
As the theater began to recover from devastating losses in the ranks of choreographers, Michael Smuin was one of the few to emerge on Broadway in the 1980s. Here, Smuin's tap dancers for the 1987 revival of Cole Porter's *Anything Goes*, staged at Lincoln Center, are led by Patti LuPone. Among the songs added from other Cole Porter shows to this already wonderful score were "It's De-Lovely" and "Friendship." Audiences did not object. Designer Tony Walton's challenge was to streamline the old scene-by-scene set changes and he did it in a dazzling exercise in Art Deco.

13

Les Misérables combined the heartiness of traditional Broadway with a contemporary quality in its music. More than any other recent musical it was responsible for returning younger audiences to the theater.

the lean years of the 1980s, the *showbiz* musicals of Broadway lost momentum. There was nothing to be enthusiastic about, and enthusiasm itself seemed only a memory. The leadership of Harold Prince and Stephen Sondheim began to wane. Impressive as their collaborations had been, something had been lacking. Audiences had pointed that out. Their series of artworks had provided no hits. Paradoxically, *A Chorus Line*, which Sondheim and Prince had *not* created, was the culmination of their work. Its director and creator, Michael Bennett, had been a protégé of Prince's, learning from him while choreographing *Company* and co-directing *Follies*. But audiences were mad for Bennett's *Chorus Line*, though they had not been remotely as enthusiastic about the Prince and Sondheim concept musicals that had given birth to it. Many knowing theatergoers admired the brilliance of these works, but not many *loved* them, and audiences are lovers, not admirers. They are rowdies in suits and dresses, and when the theatrical equation calls for a hit, the rowdies must be breaking down the doors and stomping on the floors. That had not been happening at such Sondheim-Prince shows as *Pacific Overtures* and *Sweeney Todd*. Kabuki musicals and shows about cannibalism somehow weren't setting the audiences to whoop and whistle.

Then, too, while Sondheim and Prince were doing innovative shows, Broadway's more traditional composers and lyricists seemed to be losing their audiences. This generation of well made show writers, after having supplied Broadway with two decades of high-energy, well made musicals, was responsible for virtually no hits in the 1980s. And the few such traditional musicals that did succeed were merely extravagant versions of what had once been bread-and-butter shows. Their extravagance seemed not organic but calculated to justify higher ticket prices, which had been a mere $15 when *A Chorus Line* opened. Five years later, in 1980, they soared to $35. Later in the 1980s, *Jerome Robbins' Broadway* took them to $60 and in 1990, producer Cameron Mackintosh announced a $100 top ticket for *Miss Saigon*.

Even stiffer than the price of admission was the toll being taken on atmosphere. A show seen at the cost of a week's groceries is not a show that is easily enjoyed, and even if theatergoers paid such prices for a top attraction, they would not do it for lesser shows. At such prices, too, an element of "prove it" was introduced. In short, a visit to a Broadway show became such a grotesquely expensive proposition that the pleasure of just going was threatened.

Nor did bigger musicals necessarily mean better ones. The movement toward creative staging that had been introduced by 1957's trailblazing *West Side Story*—the movement toward *concept musicals*—screeched to a halt with Michael Bennett's death in 1987, and with the decision of Stephen Sondheim and Harold Prince to separate for a time. Years of doing their best to scant public response had drained their highminded enthusiasm for these concept musicals that were so artistic a development from Broadway musical fundamentals. Left leaderless, musicals drifted into businesslike lethargy, becoming matters of investment rather than of enthusiasm and belief. Those that did succeed, having no competition, ran ever longer. Minor shows like *42nd Street* had blockbuster runs. The hit-flop syndrome, always troubling, worsened. No longer were there medium-sized successes like *The Music Man, Bye Bye Birdie,* or *Gypsy* to run a few years and become staples of the repertoire. Instead, a show like *42nd Street,* hardly in that class, could run seven years, while a perfectly enjoyable *Romance, Romance* or *The Rink* would fail. Indeed, at times, a small group of long-running shows was so entrenched that it seemed as if the only thing changing on Broadway was the audiences.

Stephen Sondheim without Harold Prince was free, for better or worse, from any imperative toward popularity, whether motivated by financial considerations, respect for the idea of a hit, or the simple needs of ego. His shows became ever brainier and emotionally remote. His style was *Broadway*, but the sound of Broadway meant heat to audiences. Prince, ironically, joined forces with Sondheim's opposite number, the passionate and popular Andrew Lloyd Webber.

Meantime, a modern-day impresario, Cameron Mackintosh, defying Prince's conviction that one man could no longer raise the money a musical had come to cost, not only did that but in the process attempted to forge a link between a new kind of music in a newer kind of musical theater (*Cats*, *Les Misérables*) and the Broadway tradition that had first attracted him — the tradition that Sondheim represented at its most refined. Mackintosh even revived Sondheim's *Follies* in London. As the composer-lyricist wrote in that magnificently unpopular 1970 show:

> Good times and bum times
> I've seen them all and, my dear,
> I'm still here

He might well have been speaking of Broadway musicals, for somehow they were surviving, their greasepaint a protection against the electrons in the air, their durability a testament to the improbable.

But it was the Mackintosh-produced shows — *Cats*, *Les Misérables*, *The Phantom of the Opera* — that brought on the change that revived Broadway. More visual and musical than verbal, his productions survived book and lyric writing that came perilously close to amateur. A Broadway accustomed to wizardly lyrics from the likes of Lorenz Hart, Ira Gershwin, Cole Porter, or more currently Fred Ebb, Sheldon Harnick, and Sondheim himself looked on in contempt — but had it not once contemptuously missed the musicals (*Hair*, *Godspell*) that had forewarned of change? Now this contempt was drenched with envy and lost in ignorance of what was happening. For the truth of the matter was that the rightness of these new shows outweighed their faults. This was new blood coursing through a tired musical theater.

In the 1980s, musicals tended to keep the curtains up at the start and audiences were deprived of the traditional and magical greeting of a curtain glowing like this one in the beautiful Royale Theatre on West 45th Street. With a seating capacity of barely over a thousand, the Royale is small for a show that costs a lot to run but, in fact, it was built for musicals. Over the years this glowing red curtain lifted the spirits of audiences leaving the workaday world to see the likes of *DuBarry Was a Lady*, *New Faces of 1952*, and *The Boy Friend*. During the 1980s there were some smaller musicals that could afford to play the Royale— *Joseph and The Amazing Technicolor Dreamcoat*, for instance, *A Day in Hollywood/A Night in the Ukraine*, and Andrew Lloyd Webber's *Song and Dance*.

17

Those who bemoaned the end of the good old days lost their battle. They were left to wring their hands, for time and change had come to provide "good old days" for the future.

Another transition was mortal. In the decade since *Broadway Musicals* was published, the theater's two remaining giants, Richard Rodgers and Irving Berlin, died, so that the last of the connections to Broadway's origins were severed. Lost, too, was the generation of great choreographer-directors who had dominated the 1960s and 1970s: Michael Bennett, Bob Fosse, and Gower Champion — the latter's death in 1980 played itself out in melodramatic style, announced by David Merrick from the stage of the Majestic Theatre on the opening night of Champion's last show and greatest hit, *42nd Street.* This dramatic moment had a double meaning, first that the era of *42nd Street*–type shows — flashy musical comedies — was at an end; second that dead, too, was the era of David Merrick, the archetypal producer of musicals. In a gesture of melancholy flamboyance, this once outrageous and indefatigable promoter had insisted on financing *42nd Street* with his own money. The sum was awesome: two million dollars.

By decade's end, it seemed paltry.

Approaching the end of the twentieth century, the musical theater is vital at a time when drama and comedy have all but disappeared from Broadway stages. Instead of Irving Berlin and Richard Rodgers, or Gower Champion, Bob Fosse, Jerome Robbins, and David Merrick, today's giants are Stephen Sondheim, Harold Prince, Tommy Tune, Andrew Lloyd Webber, Cameron Mackintosh, and a couple of Frenchmen named Claude-Michel Schönberg and Alain Boublil. They hold the keys to Broadway's future, theirs is the confidence in it, the vision of it that assures a tomorrow; no matter how high-powered the theater becomes, there is still a sense that they are not in it just for the money — not the international impresario Mackintosh, not Webber with his own producing company, not Harold Prince who seems to personify Broadway past and present, not Tommy Tune who is so showmanly he can never ever resist a request to tap dance, and certainly not Stephen Sondheim, the quintessential artist.

As *Broadway Musicals* was dedicated to the past, *More Broadway Musicals,* as its title suggests, is dedicated to survival, continuity, and the future that these people represent. Its intent is to recognize this kind of theater's improbable endurance — more Broadway musicals in an era of shuddering economic and technological transition, more Broadway musicals in continuance of tradition in an age when tradition is itself out of style, more Broadway musicals because of a childish, illogical, but persistent need to create and revel in this uniquely transporting kind of live theatrical entertainment.

It is hand made, home made, utterly anachronistic theater, reminding us that something as earthy and foolish as show business can still exist. It is showmaking that quickens the pulse and lifts the spirit, elating us in the secret dark. *More Broadway Musicals* celebrates the "more" in theater, the demand for an encore to stop the curtain from falling and to keep the chorus line kicking forever.

Michael Bennett demonstrates for a dancer how to move with a gown.

1

BROADWAY'S GREATEST HITS OF THE EIGHTIES

For a decade that set out, in terms of musicals, slogging through dire times, the 1980s provided a fair share of hits. In hindsight, that was remarkable considering that it was to be a revolutionary and sometimes painful period of transition. But change is vitality, and by the time the eighties ended, Broadway's musicals had new life.

When the decade began, *Fiddler on the Roof* held the record for the longest running show in Broadway history (3,242 performances). By 1990, no fewer than four musicals had outdistanced it: *Grease*, with 3,388 performances; *42nd Street*, with 3,485; *Cats*, with 3,300 (and still running); and of course *A Chorus Line*, which was the new champion with 6,137 performances. Plainly, musicals were running longer than they ever had.

But there is no actor as well-dressed as an unemployed one, and in a sense Broadway was putting on a bold front. For these long-running hits did not mean a thriving theater except in a financial sense. Perhaps the producers might have enjoyed a Broadway where the shows never changed and houses were always sold out, but that would have meant the death of the theater. If nothing new is being created, there is no life.

One problem was the Greatest Hits syndrome itself. Just as chain bookstores were tending to stock only those titles that were on the best seller lists, and as radio stations were tending to play only the top songs on the record charts, and just as blockbuster pictures dominated movie attendance, so Broadway was beginning to look like a list of greatest hits too. Where once there had been a menu of diverse musicals from which to choose, and where once a successful show might run a couple of seasons, a *Brigadoon* or a *Plain and Fancy* or an *Unsinkable Molly Brown*, and where once the mark of a truly great hit was a couple of thousand performances like the 2,211 of *Oklahoma!* or *My Fair Lady*'s 2,717, now such runs were commonplace. Commonplace, too, was the short life of everything else, not only of the flops but of the experimental and ambitious, the almosts and the interestings.

Gower Champion's farewell show, *42nd Street*, was virtually a nonstop succession of musical numbers. Here, Wanda Richert kicks up her heels.

The survival of those shows, the in-betweens rather than the megahits, was a lifesign of a healthy theater.

For America's own musicals, the eighties' greatest hits included one from the previous decade—*A Chorus Line*—and only two outright smashes, *42nd Street* and *La Cage aux Folles*, both of which ran for most of the decade.

These were wonderfully entertaining musicals to be sure. As Gower Champion's last stand *42nd Street* was a spectacular package. It hardly mattered that the story line from the famous movie on which it was based was only sketched out. Producer Merrick, in a gesture of grand malevolence reminiscent of his evil heyday, threatened to (and for a while did) reduce the credit of librettists Michael Stewart and Mark Bramble to "Lead-ins and Crossovers"—theatricalese for song cues and dialogue linkage between numbers. Merrick advertised the show as "a song and dance extravaganza," which is pretty much what it was—flashy musical numbers with the bones of a story just barely holding them together. That the show succeeded so well without a story structure is a measure of Gower Champion's direction, and its long run testifies to Merrick's promotional abilities. Even still, *42nd Street* would never have been launched so successfully had not Champion, melodramatically, died on the very day it opened in New York. The front-page publicity catapulted the show

Champion was trying to recover his winning touch when he created the wall-to-wall tap dancing of *42nd Street*. Here, Lee Roy Reams leads the ensemble.

Opposite:
In this sleeping car staging of "Shuffle Off to Buffalo" in *42nd Street*, Champion not only took off from Busby Berkeley's choreography for the original movie, but also his own "Telephone Hour" number from *Bye Bye Birdie*.

21

Gower Champion poses
with the *42nd Street* chorus.

to sell-out status despite mixed reviews. After that, Merrick kept *42nd Street* running for eight years on bursts of publicity that ranged from threatening to open a *second* company of the show on Broadway, to threatening to close it altogether.

Such malarkey was wonderfully reminiscent of the old days and the old hokum, but in fact *42nd Street* was not like the old shows. It was more of a big show than a great or even good one but anything could be forgiven when the chorus started tapping to the title song and when Tammy Grimes sang "You're Getting to Be a Habit With Me," or Jerry Orbach performed "Lullaby of Broadway."

La Cage aux Folles was both more and less traditional. It was constructed along the sturdy lines of the conventional, or "book" musicals (plays plus musical numbers) that had dominated Broadway since the days of Rodgers and Hammerstein, and it was directed by one of the masters of such shows, Arthur Laurents. Its composer, Jerry Herman, was one of the best among Broadway's fine professionals, and the show was an even bigger hit than such previous successes of his as *Hello, Dolly!* and *Mame*, with rousing songs in the Broadway style of which he was a master. But the show's subject was hardly traditional, dealing as it does with homosexual romance and transvestite entertainment. Laurents's careful touch and Herman's warm music led audiences to overcome prejudices and psychological barriers and take *La Cage aux Folles* to their hearts.

22

Two of the decade's successes that had real artistic merit and that were among the few to continue the development of concept musicals were *Dreamgirls* and *Nine*, and both were produced the same season (1981-82). Directed and chorographed, respectively, by Michael Bennett and his protégé Tommy Tune, they would compete for the year's Tony Award.

Dreamgirls was unique in that it continued to evolve over the course of its Broadway run as Bennett changed and improved it. The show was also modern in its frequent use of recitative as Bennett pursued the elusive goal of the all-musical musical, with song now as well as choreography. *Nine*, curiously enough, seemed *less* musical than most musicals. Its director Tommy Tune was absorbed with the visual aspects of theater, and while he was making this show a ravishing vision, he paid scant attention to choreography or even movement. But it was *Nine* that won the Tony rather than *Dreamgirls*, and the two shows introduced fresh composers to Broadway, Henry Krieger with *Dreamgirls* and Maury Yeston with *Nine*.

Other new composers arriving on Broadway during the 1980s were the country-music writer Roger Miller and the rock performer-composer Rupert Holmes. Although neither Miller's *Big River* nor Holmes's *Mystery of Edwin Drood* had the kind of smash-hit success that sets New York on its ear, both shows won Tony Awards, both were legitimate successes, and both were written by composers who were not prisoners of Broadway tradition. As a result, these two did not have the standard sound of Broadway.

An acceptance that a musical's music could be written in many styles had been overdue. The love of the long-accepted "Broadway" sound had been an impris-

Directing *La Cage aux Folles*, Arthur Laurents did not spare the glitz. He knew it was appropriate to the material. Laurents can be a cruel man to work with but professionals are grateful to have him because there are few cannier, brighter, or better directors of musicals.

This painting-like stage composition was designed for *Big River* by Heidi Landesman under Des McAnuff's direction, evoking the warmth and nostalgia of Mark Twain's *Adventures of Huckleberry Finn*, on which the show was based.

oning one, its embrace confining and stifling. The Broadway style of music could certainly continue and it could be turned to more sophisticated purposes, as Stephen Sondheim was proving. But Roger Miller demonstrated that a country style could also work, and Holmes employed a British music-hall style of number for his Dickensian *Drood*.

But of all the new musical languages being introduced, most critical was that introduced by the British invasion that scared Broadway to death while bringing it back to life. The invaders were led by Andrew Lloyd Webber, whose *Evita* began the 1980s. His *Cats* came in 1982 and several years later another blockbuster arrived, the British production of *Les Misérables*, composed by Claude-Michel Schönberg to a text by Alain Boublil. Webber's personal invasion—some on Broadway considered it an assault—also included hits that *merely* ran a year or two (*Joseph and the Amazing Technicolor Dreamcoat, Song and Dance, Starlight Express*), but he closed out the decade in spectacular style as *The Phantom of the Opera* played to stupendous audience response and then began the 1990s with *Aspects of Love*. Meantime another juggernaut could be heard on the way, *Miss Saigon*, from the authors of *Les Misérables*, and due in New York in April, 1991.

Theatergoers who lined up in hope of *Phantom of the Opera* cancellations at the Majestic Theatre became a nightly phenomenon along West 44th Street. Indeed, producer David Merrick delayed the curtain of his *42nd Street* by half an hour after the Webber show began, just so that disappointed *Phantom*-eers could cross the street and buy tickets to his musical at the St. James Theatre.

But the British brought more than popular new musicals. They brought confidence and belief, their enthusiasm shaming the defeatism and lethargy among America's musical creators. Even an old British show, the 1930s musical comedy *Me and My Girl*, enraptured Broadway audiences. Had this ever been a great show? In an era of Rodgers and Hart and Jerome Kern, these songs by Noel Gay could not compare. But the endlessly repeated "Lambeth Walk" was positively delicious, and so was the spirit of this lightly self-mocking production. Audiences were enchanted by the warmth of the show, its loving comedy highlighted by the kind of star performance, Robert Lindsay's, that had seemed to die with Ethel Merman, Robert Preston, and Yul Brynner.

This revival of *Me and My Girl* was a triumph of style, the production's attitude nostalgic and disarming. Without a doubt the potential of its star role and the charm of those who played it (whether Lindsay or Jim Dale, his successor) were elements essential to the show's popularity. Cole Porter's *Anything Goes* is a similar musical comedy of the period, with a libretto so inane that revivals have been all but impossible. Although its score is incomparably superior no star performance can rescue it from the script because the leading role is a singer (in the original production, Ethel Merman) and no singer can save a show anymore.

But with the script rewritten and set askew by the gifted playwright John Weidman (*Pacific Overtures*) in collaboration with Timothy Crouse (whose father, Russell, had written the original libretto with Howard Lindsay), *Anything Goes* became the American match for *Me and My Girl*. Zestfully directed by Jerry Zaks and designed by Tony Walton so stylishly that it could be loved for its looks alone, the revival was a two-year hit at Lincoln Center, enchanting audiences with its array

Bernadette Peters in the *Song* section of Webber's *Song and Dance*. She and Patti LuPone took the juiciest female leads in the period's musicals.

The new version of *The Pirates of Penzance* was born at the New York Shakespeare Festival's free outdoor Delacorte Theater in Central Park. Here, Kevin Kline *(left center)* rehearses as the Pirate King.

Opposite:
Robert Lindsay brought an aristocratic slapstick to his performance in *Me and My Girl*, vaulting over the sofa if beauty beckoned or dancing with the aristocratically delicious George S. Irving.

of Cole Porter classics including "You're the Top," "I Get a Kick Out of You," "Blow, Gabriel, Blow," "Anything Goes," and a restored "Easy to Love," which had been deleted from the original production because William Gaxton couldn't hit the high notes. The revival ran longer than the Broadway original had. It established Zaks as an important and badly needed new director of musicals.

A suprise hit from yet another institutional theater was a tongue-in-cheek version of the (itself tongue-in-cheek) Gilbert and Sullivan classic *The Pirates of Penzance*, featuring rock star Linda Ronstadt and a thoroughly risky and brazen comic performance by the young and relatively unknown Kevin Kline. As the Pirate King willing to trade swordplay with the pit conductor and his baton, Kline typified the show's antic spirit. Once again, audiences were proving their openness to fresh ideas, an openness frankly greater than that of most producers.

A fresh idea of Stephen Sondheim's gave him his greatest success as a composer since 1962's *A Funny Thing Happened on the Way to the Forum*. This was *Into the Woods*, a collaboration with librettist-director James Lapine that played on the

light and the dark sides of fairy tales, from *Cinderella* to *Jack and the Beanstalk* and *Little Red Riding Hood*. Sondheim's other success of the decade, *Sunday in the Park with George*, was more cerebral. That, perhaps, was why it lost the 1984 Tony Award to the less ambitious but warmer-hearted *La Cage aux Folles*. The Sondheim shows established Lapine as the decade's other new director of musicals.

As the 1980s drew to a close, however, it became clear that these American shows had not carried the times but, rather, survived them. The British were not taking over our musical theater really, although they were opening its eyes to possibilities for growth. The tremendous audience response to *Cats* and the rest was a statement that the time for a different and more contemporary kind of music in a different and more contemporary musical theater had arrived; not that musical comedy or concept musicals had seen their last but that Broadway no longer could be monopolized with formula showmaking by a small group of insiders.

In a way, Broadway's own conceded as much when their best musical of 1988 turned out to be a revival. The greatest of all choreographer-directors Jerome Robbins had been coaxed out of retirement, but the newest he could do was *Jerome*

Robbins' Broadway, a compendium of numbers from old musicals stretching back to the forties (*High Button Shoes*) and fifties (*The King and I*). Critics were fooled but audiences weren't.

With its new so old, Broadway's future seemed at graveside. It was the British, still lovestruck by musical comedy and not yet jaded, who returned its gifts by yanking it back to life. Instead of clinging to an archaic musical-comedy language of the past, with its adorable but half-century-old style of show tunes, these new musicals introduced a modern sensibility in music and showmaking.

Unlike Broadway's occasional newcomer-composer who would fling himself into a Richard Rodgers or Frank Loesser mode when writing for the stage, the British and French writers were not bound to Broadway tradition. They sensed the excitement of its potential but wrote for today's theater and today's audiences.

Thanks to them, Broadway is again growing. Perhaps it was necessary, even inevitable, that outsiders would recover the enthusiasm that had always been at the heart of our musicals. The shows like *Cats* and *Les Miz* by the British and French did

Producer David Merrick has a lifetime of great hits. When he produced a revival of George and Ira Gershwin's *Oh, Kay!* in 1990, he locked the theater doors during previews, refunded tickets, and sat alone in the theater to judge its readiness. Despite such attention to detail (and the publicity that resulted), the show failed.

In the 1980s Japan became the third major market for Broadway musicals. Theaters of two and three thousand seats, in Osaka as well as Tokyo, began to resound with brassy overtures. Audiences thronged to world-famous new shows like *Cats*, *Les Misérables*, and *Phantom of the Opera*. *Opposite:* This 1986 revival of *West Side Story* originated in Osaka. The actors playing the gang were made up to look western, with their hair bleached and curled. But Japan's favorite musical was *Fiddler on the Roof*, performed in Japanese. *Above:* Hisaya Morishige makes his third (and final) appearance as Tevya.

Above right:
Jerome Robbins works with dancers on his reprise show *Jerome Robbins Broadway*.

Overleaf:
A curtain call reveals all the musicals that make up the show.

not mean the end of *Guys and Dolls* — only the end of *Guys and Dolls Forever*, and with it, the start of new life. Provoked, our own artists have begun to grow fertile once more, and to thrive. As the 1990s arrived, so did hit shows as diverse as *Grand Hotel* — a landmark concept musical — and the hilarious musical comedy *City of Angels*. They were shows created out of conviction and enthusiasm, shows made for the love of it. The magic of musicals, having enchanted Europeans, was returned in gratitude and just in time.

2
STEPHEN SONDHEIM

Stephen Sondheim's 1980s began with a revival of his first Broadway credit, *West Side Story,* and ended with a revival of his second, *Gypsy,* and a painful irony lay between those theatrical book ends. For by 1990, thirteen shows into the game, after a Pulitzer Prize and countless Tony Awards — without a doubt a composer in a class by himself, to be ranked with the giants of the musical theater — Sondheim still seemed dogged by his youthful successes and by his role in them as strictly a lyricist. *West Side Story* and *Gypsy* were simply more popular than his music-and-lyrics shows, and Sondheim knew the significance of popularity on Broadway; moreover, he knew that significance to be not merely financial but symbolic. For he had grown up under the influence of Oscar Hammerstein II, was professionally parented by the commercial theater, and had early fallen in love with the excitement of Broadway musicals. He knew the tough rules of that game, the first of them being that Broadway is about hits.

Sondheim could never disdain this commercial stage he yearned to conquer and he would always be the first to respect professionalism, the last to be a theater snob. Yet just after the March, 1979 premiere of his *Sweeney Todd, the Demon Barber of Fleet Street,* he ruefully observed, "I'm still essentially a cult figure. My kind of work is just too unexpected for the general public. . . . The only really popular show I've ever had is *A Funny Thing Happened on the Way to the Forum.*"

There seemed to be more than a trace of melancholy in the remarks.

Oddly enough, *Sweeney Todd* was almost continuously performed in New York during the 1980s, first throughout a 557-performance Broadway engagement, and then in repertory at the New York City Opera, ending the decade in a successful chamber-sized revival at the Circle in the Square that, coincidentally, sits just downstairs from the theater where the show had opened in the first place.

Yet, despite these productions *Sweeney Todd* still seemed a cult musical. Broadway has come far since the carefree and brainless *Very Good Eddie* by Jerome Kern, or George Gershwin's *Tip-Toes,* but for all the progress, even modern hits like

The demon barber *Sweeney Todd* (Len Cariou) repays Judge Turpin (Edmund Lyndeck).

My Fair Lady, A Chorus Line, or The Phantom of the Opera have a euphoria about them. Indeed, no matter how highly developed Broadway musicals may become, they will always be rooted in passionate, emotional, populist theater, and there will always be a need to make the audience gulp and chill before they go out whistling the tunes.

These are effects that Sondheim shuns, never more successfully, as it were, than in Sweeney Todd. The problem about the show seems to be: if it doesn't stimulate emotional heat, then what is its theatrical purpose? To, as Sondheim suggests, give a good scare? To, as director Harold Prince suggests, just be campy? The show seems to do itself very well, but just what it is doing by that is never clear. It is a formidable work with plain lasting power, but it is a problematic work.

Sweeney Todd, the Demon Barber of Fleet Street is based on a story that appeared in a British "penny dreadful" (pulp horror book) published in 1846. Sondheim, visiting London in 1973, saw a dramatization of the tale by playwright Christopher Bond and suggested to Prince that it be the basis of their next musical collaboration. Thus it became the first of their works to originate with Sondheim. Until then he had been concentrating on the musical part of the showmaking process, but now this collaborator was budding as a complete man of the theater.

Hugh Wheeler, who was engaged to write the libretto — what little of it would be spoken — kept close to the original plot. This tells of the barber Sweeney Todd, whose real name is Benjamin Barker, returning from a wrongful imprisonment that had been imposed on him by the corrupt Judge Turpin. With Barker locked away, the judge had seduced the barber's wife and, while she sank into madness, took their daughter Johanna as his ward. Now Barker has returned, crazed for revenge. He sets up a barber shop with the intention of slaughtering anyone under his razor, especially Judge Turpin. Downstairs, meanwhile, his landlady, Mrs. Lovett, runs a meat-pie shop and, herself somewhat mad, upon discovering Todd's murderous style, she suggests that they grind up his victims and bake them into pies.

> Have a bit of priest
> It's too good
> At least
> Then again, they don't commit sins of the flesh
> So it's pretty fresh

Thus the Grand Guignol musical that Sondheim had in mind, but — bloody revenge carried out by a couple of near lunatics — was that a sufficient purpose for a musical? Director Harold Prince had such worries. In production he provided theatrical size with a gigantic set (in fact, a real factory carted in its entirety from New England); even still the show was dominated by music, two hours of nearly continuous music, by far the most ambitious, the most serious, of Sondheim's career.

Despite the ghoulish subject, much of the music is rapturous — the yearning love song "Johanna," for instance, or the lyrical and touching "Not While I'm Around." In a surprising way, the start of the show is a standard Broadway opening number, although hardly of the Oklahoma! variety. Sondheim knows the importance of starting a show right: an opening should tell the audience what to expect. "The Ballad of Sweeney Todd" does exactly that, from its piercing factory whistle and horror-movie organ chords to the ballad itself, its musical tone and its words:

Attend the tale of Sweeney Todd
His skin was pale and his eye was odd
He shaved the faces of gentlemen
Who never thereafter were heard of again
Did Sweeney Todd
The Demon Barber of Fleet Street

There are also more conventional numbers, for notwithstanding Sondheim's high aims, his music does tend to be in the Broadway vernacular. Typical of these is "Pirelli's Miracle Elixir," in which a competing barber gives Sweeney Todd the chance to show off his tonsorial skills while Sondheim flaunts a parallel rhyming prowess. He matches "elixir" with "trick, sir," "quick, sir," "wick, sir," and "nick, sir."

But rhyming is only the flashiest of his lyric-writing talents. Sondheim has consistently furthered Oscar Hammerstein's notion of lyricized dramatic scenes. This blend of song and drama is at its most advanced in *Sweeney Todd*. Conversational language is never mere dialogue; it is lyrical, being metric and stylized, grander in expression than ordinary language. Not for Sondheim the recitative of opera, with everyday conversation set to sing-song music.

When the dialogue does evolve into a set piece, a formal song, Sondheim's lyrics continue to be conversational even while poetic.

No one's gonna hurt you
No one's gonna dare
Others can desert you

38

Not to worry
Whistle, I'll be there

To hear the familiar turn of phrase anew, the ascent of the ordinary to the extraordinary, that is the test of the poet's ear. Sondheim has always been acutely sensitive to poetry in the colloquial, whether it is a phrase such as "not to worry" or "whistle, I'll be there," or the straight, streetcorner style used by Mama Rose in *Gypsy*.

Now's your inning
Stand the world on its ear
Set it spinning
That'll be just the beginning

Every word in this section (the song's middle part or "release" coming after the main "chorus") is in Rose's vernacular, simple and direct. The triple rhyming of "inning," "spinning" and "beginning" never preens in its own brilliance. Sondheim learned from Oscar Hammerstein to care only that the rhyming works for subliminal musical and rhythmic purposes. In addition, he means that "Everything's Coming Up Roses" in two senses—everything will be rosy and the future looks filled with Roses, Gypsy and her mother. He is also extending librettist Arthur Laurents' overall theme of Rose and her dreams in his verse (or introduction) for the song.

I had a dream
I dreamed it for you, baby
It's gonna come true, baby
They think that we're through, but baby

And that, incidentally, involves still more triple rhymes, feminine ones at that because they rhyme on inner syllables—"you, baby," "true, baby," and "through, baby."

Sweeney Todd had closed the 1970s as Sondheim's fifth show of that decade. He would write only three musicals in the 1980s, which probably was more a matter of Broadway economics than of abating energies. Those were *Merrily We Roll Along*, *Sunday in the Park With George* and *Into The Woods* (he would begin his 1990s in 1991, with the one act, off-Broadway *Assassins*).

The fortunes of these Broadway shows ranged from the pathetic sixteen performances of *Merrily We Roll Along* to the 764 played by *Into The Woods*, making it Sondheim's biggest hit since the 964 performances of *A Funny Thing Happened on the Way to the Forum* (both *Forum* and *Into the Woods*, incidentally, ran longer than either *Gypsy* or *West Side Story*).

But if the success of *Into the Woods* should have been cheering, there remains an undertone of resentment in Sondheim's reactions to the popularity of his early shows. He repeatedly knocks his *West Side Story* lyrics ("Say it soft and it's almost like praying") and after the reception given the Tyne Daly revival of *Gypsy* in 1989, the only pride he could muster for a *New York Times* interview was to call his powerful and perfect lyrics for the show "neat" (as in tidy).

Critical of others and mordant about himself, Stephen Sondheim is surely weary of a prime identification with these first works. He ranks with Broadway's greatest and most important composers. His scores are not merely entertaining with

Tyne Daly (right) appeared with Crista Moore as Louise, soon to become Gypsy Rose Lee, in the successful 1989 revival of the Jule Styne–Arthur Laurents–Stephen Sondheim classic. Below, one of the strippers shows her "gimmick".

ingenious and eloquent lyrics set to rich, idiosyncratic music; they are integral to a series of major stage works, each pursuing a new and challenging ambition. It is true that the public has not responded to his songs with the affection given composers from Irving Berlin to Andrew Lloyd Webber, but Sondheim seems almost deliberately to avoid such popularity. Burton Lane, one of Broadway's masters *(Finian's Rainbow, On a Clear Day You Can See Forever)*, said of Sondheim's lone popular song, "If Steve had known that 'Send in the Clowns' was going to be a hit, he would have cut it from *A Little Night Music*."

Yet anyone attending various professional workshops for composers and lyricists is familiar with the inspiration that he has provided for young writers. Only his mentor, Oscar Hammerstein II, has comparably contributed to the progress of Broadway musicals.

Why, then, is his appeal so limited? Is it because, as he says, his work is so "unexpected"? (The implication is that audiences like only the familiar, which is not true, since *A Chorus Line, Cats,* and *Les Misérables* are not traditional musicals.) Or is

Above, and opposite: For *Into the Woods,* the design of sets (Tony Straiges) and costumes (Ann Hould-Ward) reflected the desire of Stephen Sondheim and James Lapine to capture both the dark and light of fairy tales — the adult in them and the childlike. The leading players from *Into the Woods* were Bernadette Peters, Joanna Gleason, Chip Zien, Robert Westenberg, and Tom Aldredge.

41

Audiences at *Merrily We Roll Along* were so confused that the actors were given sweatshirts with their characters' names stencilled on.

Sondheim's appeal limited because musicals are an affirmative and emotional theater and his own shows are so cerebral, so reflective of a sour view of life? For that matter, has he lost his leadership of the musical theater to the more open-hearted and flamboyant Andrew Lloyd Webber? There is a real question of whether Sondheim's influence on the direction of our musical theater has waned after the stunning series of concept musicals that he created with Harold Prince during the 1970s — *Company, Follies, A Little Night Music, Pacific Overtures,* and *Sweeney Todd.*

There are other questions as the 1990s begin: how has the professional separation from Prince affected his work? And finally, if Sondheim is the master of the production-oriented concept musical and Andrew Lloyd Webber the prime developer of the musically dominated, entirely sung, through-composed show, in which direction does the future of Broadway musicals lie? One thing is certain: nobody on Broadway ever caught the spirit of artistic idealism as Stephen Sondheim has, and he has done it with professionalism and nobility.

Perhaps it was Sondheim's greater role in the creation of *Sweeney Todd* that led him to break with Prince, seeking to express his own choices; perhaps both men felt that a vacation might be salutary; but the catalyst for the actual rupture, apparently, was the failure of their only 1980s collaboration, *Merrily We Roll Along.*

Reuniting the *Company* team of Sondheim, Prince, and librettist George Furth, this musical seemed to be an attempt at something light, after the esoteric *Pacific Overtures* and *Sweeney Todd.* It emerged as Sondheim's first critical disaster since *Anyone Can Whistle.* Based on a flop comedy by George S. Kaufman and Moss Hart, *Merrily* adopted the play's conceit of starting in the present and going backwards as it traces the career of a rich and famous songwriter. Beginning with his cynical advice to a high-school graduating class on the need for compromise, the story concludes as he gives an idealistic valedictorian address twenty-five years earlier to his own class at the same school. Thus, the show finds the road to success paved with betrayals of talent and friends.

Were Sondheim and Prince making a show about themselves, two friends and collaborators falling away from each other because one (Prince) is a realist and the other an idealist? Harold Prince is an intensely principled man but he is a pragmatist as well. It might have been that his origins as a producer and his theatrical apprenticeship to another of Broadway's great pragmatists, George Abbott, made him hungrier than Sondheim for audience approval.

The musical approach in *Merrily We Roll Along* is typical of Sondheim's braininess. The style of the music and lyrics is fitted to each period covered by the show, reaching back to the Kennedy era and then altering with every time change. "Since the story moves backward in time," he writes, "verbal and musical motifs... could be modified over the course of the years, extended and developed, reprised, fragmented, and then presented to the audience in reverse...in fact, if the score is listened to in reverse order — although it wasn't written that way — it develops traditionally."

Such tortuous reasoning is a typical Sondheim brainscreen, a wall of reason behind which emotions can be hidden just as, so often, his rich melodies lurk behind nasty or smirking tones of voice. But his melodies *are* rich, and the emotion is most certainly there. It is difficult to imagine a more sympathetic and eloquent expression about hurt, or dark expectations more typical of Sondheim, than this from *Merrily We Roll Along:*

> All right, now you know
> Life is crummy
> Well, now you know
>
> It's called flowers wilt,
> It's called apples rot,
> It's called thieves get rich and saints get shot
> It's called God don't answer prayers a lot
> Okay, now you know
>
> Yes sir, quite a blow
> Don't regret it,
> And don't let's go to extremes
> It's called what's your choice?
> It's called count to ten
> It's called burn your bridges, start again,
> You should burn them every now and then
> Or you'll never grow!
>
> You're right, nothing's fair
> And it's all a plot
> And tomorrow doesn't look so hot
> Right, you better look at what you've got
> Over here, hello?

The brilliance of these lyrics is not merely in subtle rhymes, ingeniously schemed, but in an attitude that is captured through colloquial expressions. Again, as in *Sweeney Todd*, ordinary phrases such as "it's called," "don't let's go to extremes," "over here, hello?" or casually poor grammar ("God don't answer prayers a lot") or conversational English like, "Right, you better look at what you've got," are raised above mere argot. Everyday language becomes, well, *lyrical*, and all to the precise meter of his music. This is a work of poetry, craftsmanlike and controlled.

The score for *Merrily* is in the Broadway style and yet it is musicianly — catchy, funny, elating, and touching. It is probably the best generic *Broadway* score of the decade. One sequence is particularly relevant to Sondheim because it is personal: in an ingenious musical-dramatic collage, the show's composer and his lyricist-friend audition their musical for a producer who responds in the way so many in the music and theater businesses have responded to Sondheim scores.

> That's great
> That's swell
> The other stuff as well
> It isn't everyday I hear a score this strong
> But fellas, if I may
> There's only one thing wrong
> There's not a tune you can hum

The producer is not only off-key when he sings "hum," but makes his exit humming "Some Enchanted Evening," the kind of tune-you-can-hum that Sondheim loves to deride, especially since it was written by his *bête noire*, Richard Rodgers.

Perhaps it was from this experience with autobiographical references that the even more personal *Sunday in the Park with George* followed in 1984. Although it was with this show that the Sondheim-Prince divorce became final, the two old friends had been separating ever since Prince directed *Evita* in London in 1978. If he had any yearnings for a commercial hit, Prince certainly fulfilled them with *Evita*, and without artistic compromise. But if the epic approach that Prince brought to next year's *Sweeney Todd* originated in the awesome staging of the Andrew Lloyd Webber show, Sondheim moved in just the opposite direction when he next went off-Broadway and joined with writer-director James Lapine to develop the chamber-sized musical *Sunday in the Park with George*.

The Lapine-Sondheim project involved a tantalizing idea. With the central character a painter, Lapine could draw on his background as an artist while Sondheim had an opportunity to write about himself as a creator who needs and demands that he be allowed to go his own way. (As Georges Seurat says in the show, "I wanted to get through to something new. A kind of painting that was my own.") To fill out the one-act musical about Seurat's painting *A Sunday Afternoon on the Island of La Grande Jatte*, Lapine wrote a second act even more personally relevant to Sondheim, dealing with a fictitious great-grandson of Seurat who is a modern sound-and-light sculptor living in an art world dependent on museums and foundations for funding. Like a high-minded Broadway composer, he cannot do his art without financial support. Sondheim may have leaned a bit heavily on the dual meanings of the word "composition," but he certainly got his point across.

> Lining up the funds but in addition
> Lining up a prominent commission
> Otherwise your perfect composition
> Isn't going to get much exhibition

But even as *Sunday in the Park with George* was moving to Broadway, Andrew Lloyd Webber had arrived once more, and his *Cats* was an even greater success than *Evita*. Worse, *Cats* was *beloved*. Sondheim wrote into *George*

> Overnight you're a trend
> You're the right combination
> Then the trend's at an end
> You're suddenly last year's sensation

While he made little effort to conceal his contempt for Webber's work, Sondheim's *Sunday in the Park with George* won the Pulitzer Prize and, for a time, *The New York Times* seemed to be the show's press agent. But for all the prestige and publicity, *Sunday in the Park* wasn't a full-out hit; it wasn't *popular*. It was admired but not beloved. Once again, Sondheim was getting high grades. But in show business, as he knew better than anyone, the real grades were handed out at the box office, where compliments were paid by the gross.

What, then, was Broadway to make of the cult event of Sondheim's decade, the black-tie gala concert version of *Follies* at Lincoln Center's Avery Fisher Hall in 1985? And what did that event say about its composer being exalted for a show that,

Above:
Director Harold Prince's inclination was to give *Merrily We Roll Along* a spartan look. A fear that audiences expect something material for the hefty ticket prices led to costuming that in the end proved neither splashy nor simple enough.

Right:
Bernadette Peters, perhaps too coyly named Dot, moons over Mandy Patinkin, playing the Pointillist painter Georges Seurat in *Sunday in the Park with George*. Patinkin and Peters were among the new stars to emerge in the 1980s, she appearing in Andrew Lloyd Webber's *Song and Dance* as well as in Sondheim's *Into the Woods,* while Patinkin appeared in *Evita* as well as performed solo. The difference between the new stars and the old was in acting ability (a gain of it) and charisma (a loss of it).

A lovely tableau from *Sunday in the Park* shows Seurat's masterpiece nearly completed.

Late in *Sunday in the Park,* the contemporary artist played by Mandy Patinkin contemplates in a museum his great-grandfather Seurat's masterpiece, *A Sunday Afternoon on the Island of La Grande Jatte.*

James Lapine directed *Sunday in the Park.*

by the standards of the commercial theater, had been a flop because it failed to recoup its investment, 522 performances notwithstanding? Ghostly awesome as *Follies* had been in its original 1971 production, and however fabulous had been the original staging by Harold Prince and Michael Bennett, and no matter how ingenious and ingratiating Sondheim's music and lyrics were, the show committed Broadway's essential crime by losing dollars. That fact underlined the emotional excesses attending the Lincoln Center gala, reducing this inspired, landmark, musical to a mockery of its own artistry. *Follies* became the Judy Garland of musicals.

At times, Sondheim seems to accept such cultism as his lot, and at others he seems to respect Broadway's rule of popularity, hoping to succeed at it one day, his way. If his work is to be understood, this duality must be taken into account. His is at once the work of a professional and of an artist, of a man of Broadway and of an altruist. Taken in that light, the long run of *Into the Woods* should have pleased him, and in many ways this show resembled his wonderful (and popular) *A Funny Thing Happened on the Way to the Forum* — in its tongue-in-cheek innocence, its cartoon style, and its release of Sondheim's rare sense of humor. But when he wrote the songs for *Forum,* he had four very funny writers as inspiration: the original sources, Plautus and Terence, and the witty librettists Larry Gelbart and Burt Shevelove. *Forum* thus had the blessing of high-spirited scholarliness, while *Into the Woods* took its fairy tales and itself more seriously.

In its first half, the show mixes charming princes with assorted Rapunzels and Cinderellas, just barely skirting the coy. In the second act, it seeks out the dark part of the woods. In his lyrics, Sondheim is by turns upsetting

> How do you ignore
> All the witches
> All the curses
> All the wolves, all the lies
> The false hopes, the goodbyes
> The reverses?

or instructional

> Children may not obey
> But children will listen
> Children will look to you
> For which way to turn
> To learn what to be

and sometimes too tricky for words

> Not forgetting
> The tasks unachievable
> Mountains unscalable —
> If it's conceivable
> But unavailable.

Perhaps this was one show in which he let his lyrics run too fast along the byways of wizardry. There are several songs so intricately set as to be unfollowable without the printed lyrics. Also, the music for the show, while often delightful, is not stylistically consistent. There are different Sondheims in it, reminders of *Forum, Company, A Little Night Music,* and *Follies.*

Comparing his shows done with Lapine against those with Prince, the two most noticeable differences are the physical productions and the music. Both directors are very pictorial, but Lapine's interest lies in the look of scenery and costumes while Prince is more concerned with theater devices—his tools are lighting and bold production effects. Sondheim seemed to find a musical identity, or signature, for each Prince show and to create a score consistent within that identity. Working with Lapine, there is a greater emphasis on the lyrics, the music becoming a canvas on which to paint the words.

As a new decade began, Sondheim was again considering the possibility of a show with Prince, but his more immediate project was a musical to be directed by Jerry Zaks, who had staged the immensely stylish and popular revival of *Anything Goes* at Lincoln Center. Opening off-Broadway early in 1991, the ninety-minute *Assassins* was typical of the *ever predictable, ever conventional* Sondheim, a musical he described as being "about American assassins—people who tried to kill the president." It isn't as if he were unaware of his unlikely choices. With typically sardonic humor he once suggested as an opening line for a review of *Pacific Overtures:* "Oh, no! Not another kabuki musical!" As much could be said of *Assassins*, which, coincidentally enough, had a libretto written by the author of *Pacific Overtures*, John Weidman.

Such subjects, like the cannibalism in *Sweeney Todd* or the kabuki of *Pacific Overtures*, seem almost perversely chosen for commercial unattractiveness. Of course that is not really the case but, rather, these subjects represent the views and moods of this glitteringly dark composer. The moroseness and gloom that pervade his work are sad indeed, and while he meticulously justifies his attitudes in every show, audiences understandably feel the chill of his protected heart. Perhaps it is not fair to ask Stephen Sondheim to sing out, if that is not his inclination, but the musical theater that he knows and loves so well is a theater of emotional availability. Perhaps, to psychologize with caution, that is the quality that attracted Sondheim, the quality he sought to get *from* it. And considering how much Stephen Sondheim has given to the musical stage, it is not too much to ask.

The 1991 *Assassins* by Stephen Sondheim took for its subject matter the freaks and misfits in America's history who had attempted presidential assassinations. The script was written by John Weidman and the production was directed by the gifted Jerry Zaks.

Sondheim's songs were especially successful at a favorite irony, the cheerful tune for the evil mind. But the offensiveness of a song and dance Lee Harvey Oswald could not be overlooked and for the first time in a long time, a Sondheim show was savaged by the New York critics. But *Assassins* demonstrated that at the age of 60, Stephen Sondheim was as young and bold and musically adventurous as ever. Indeed, never more was his importance so evident—his nerve, courage, and willingness (even eagerness) to dare conventions and risk all in search of an artistic musical theater.

3
ANDREW LLOYD WEBBER

"I hate the division between musical theater
and opera. They're really the same."

Andrew Lloyd Webber was a virtual unknown when *Evita* opened on Broadway in September of 1979, but in the decade ahead he would rescue our musical theater from doldrums born of intimidating economics, committee producing, artistic stagnation, and lost passion. Rediscovering the enthusiasm and joy that first won the public heart for musical comedy, Webber added romance to his rapturous melodies, music that, like his theatrical ideas, did not flinch from sentiment or the grand gesture. His music soared, his shows had sweep, and audiences responded enthusiastically. The composer—the first to dominate thoroughly the creative process—came to bestride Broadway with six consecutive hits in the 1980s, three of them mammoth ones: *Evita, Cats,* and *The Phantom of the Opera.* By the time he turned forty in 1988, he was at the center of the musical stage, a stage that no longer was merely Broadway's or America's but was now international. Only Rodgers and Hammerstein had achieved such success in so brief a time.

But even while the theatergoing public was embracing Andrew Lloyd Webber's musicals, many critics disputed his talent, questioned his originality, and even protested the popularity of his shows, as if audiences were wrong for enjoying them. Despite his productivity and consistency he was accused of being a lucky success, and even his audience was denigrated, its motives and taste questioned. Satisfying an audience—which is the purpose of a commercial theater and the motivating force of Broadway musicals—never was proof of greatness, but it now was being looked upon as proof of mediocrity. In truth, ignoring an audience's taste is the first step toward emptying a theater.

Some of this hostility seemed to stem from envy, particularly of Webber's vast income; but much of it, too, seemed jingoistic, resentment of an Englishman who had mastered an American specialty. Ironically, even British critics shared that attitude. "We British had been told at birth," Webber himself said, "that we couldn't

Betty Buckley
as Grizabella
sang the big song
"Memory" in *Cats.*

Andrew Lloyd Webber is one of the rare Broadway composers who was schooled as a musician.

do musicals at all." Many of them evidently still believed it, yet not only was this Englishman atop Broadway, he was revising the holy musical writ of *Oklahoma!* and *My Fair Lady,* and that was a big reason for the outrage and the antagonism. Webber was replacing traditional show tunes with a vocabulary of opera, operetta, period, popular, and Latin music, and an occasional dash of rock-and-roll. His composing was tonal, with strong melodic lines and extensive use of lush harmonic resolutions, but he was also comfortable with dissonance and aware of its strengths. This melange of approaches had a consistency of sensibility which appealed to audiences long estranged from the theater, but which baffled aficionados. The bafflement was expressed through anger. He was accused of imitating classical composers, and some of his more ardent ballads ("Memory" from *Cats* in particular) were indeed reminiscent of Puccini, whom Webber unabashedly admired.

It is hardly unusual for one Broadway song to be reminiscent of, or even briefly sound like, another. Songwriters have hundreds of old tunes running through their heads as they write new ones, and on quite innocent occasions, a phrase from one of those tunes emerges on their keyboards. When they realize it, they invariably drop it, but they don't always realize it. That does not mean that Cy Coleman took "Real Live Girl" from Sigmund Romberg's "Stout-Hearted Men," that John Kander took "Cabaret" from Charles Strouse's "Put on a Happy Face," or that Andrew Lloyd Webber took "The Music and the Night" from Frederick Loewe's "Come to Me, Bend to Me." Accusing composers of such tune-lifting simply ignores the vast remainder of their music.

As for general reminders of another's music, trained composers are invariably influenced by predecessors. Webber admires Prokofiev as well as Puccini and is influenced by both of them, just as Stephen Sondheim's music evokes Bernstein and Ravel, or as Bernstein himself drew from Stravinsky and Copland. Even Mozart was influenced by Haydn, and Beethoven by Mozart. A composer might even be measured by the level of his influences, but whoever the influence, a true composer finds his own voice, and Webber found his. His music sounds like his music, an occasional Puccini sob notwithstanding.

He was not the first innovative stage composer subjected to abuse. Leonard Bernstein's magnificent score for *West Side Story* jarred the ears of many who felt that Broadway musicals were supposed to have a bouncy sound. Stephen Sondheim, after his first few shows, was advised to quit trying to compose music and concentrate on writing lyrics. His wonderful score for *A Funny Thing Happened on the Way to the Forum* was not even *nominated* for a Tony Award, although the show itself won it. Of course Bernstein and Sondheim were ultimately vindicated and so will Webber be.

Andrew Lloyd Webber showed an interest in the musical stage as an eight-year-old growing up in London, building a model theater and writing, as he remembers, "five terrible musicals in one year, from *The Importance of Being Earnest* to *Lady Macbeth.*" All of this came under the supervision of his father, William Lloyd Webber, who was Director of Composition at The Royal College of Music and who encouraged the boy to study counterpoint, harmony, theory, and orchestration.

As a teen-ager smitten with the rocking of Elvis Presley, the youngster met the slightly (three years) older Timothy Rice, who was a budding lyricist. The pair set out to write a musical comedy, *The Likes of Us*, frankly modeled on *Oliver!*, which was one of the rare British musicals to have succeeded on Broadway. Because of it, Webber frankly conceded, "we were all writing about jolly Cockneys."

Although their show was never produced, the head of the music department at the small Colet Court School in London was impressed and asked the young songwriters if they might work up a new piece for his choir. They turned out a fifteen-minute rock-and-roll version of the Biblical story of Joseph and his coat of many colors. Entitled *Joseph and the Amazing Technicolor Dreamcoat*, it was a naive work, devoted to rock-and-roll, but there is a youthful exuberance about it and a natural theatricality.

By the kind of chance that seems inevitable in hindsight, present among the parents at the Colet Court School premiere of *Joseph* on March 1, 1968, was a critic from the *London Sunday Times*. As Webber not so vaguely recalled, the critic wrote "a quite nice paragraph" in the *Times*. He could hardly have imagined that it would be one of the few quite nice paragraphs any critic was going to write about him during a decade of stupendous success.

Unlike most musicals Webber's *Jesus Christ Superstar* was given a different staging whenever it was produced: this is the London version.

With repeated performances of *Joseph*, more songs were added, eventually expanding the little cantata to fifty minutes' length. It was impertinent ("Poor, Poor Pharaoh"), sometimes repetitiously so ("Go, Go, Go, Joseph"), but the manner was endearing and the melodies catchy enough to win the boys a recording. Its success inspired a second Biblical piece.

If *Joseph and the Amazing Technicolor Dreamcoat* had been sassy, then *Jesus Christ Superstar* (which the spunky Rice suggested calling simply *Jesus!*) was positively outrageous. It portrayed the last seven days of Christ's life, set to rock-and-roll. Half-way through, the young team decided to aim for not the concert hall but the stage. "The backbone of any musical," Webber already knew, "is its story," and there was no story as vivid or well-known as the last days of Christ. Webber would later resolve that the plots he preferred were ones the audience knew in advance or that were at least simple enough to give the big musical numbers ample freedom. Also, even this early in the game, he was taking a novel approach to musical theater. Rather than "spotting" songs at likely moments in the script, usually at emotional climaxes, he composed his score to a general outline of the plot, writing the music before the script existed; and it was *continuous* music, for he meant every line of the dialogue to be sung. Thus were reflected his two loves, postwar Broadway musicals and grand opera.

Joseph dons his amazing Technicolor dreamcoat.

He was also outgrowing rock-and-roll. *Jesus Christ Superstar*'s music was more diverse and ambitious than *Joseph*'s, sometimes symphonic and occasionally even grandiose, especially in the orchestrations, which Webber himself wrote. That was all but unheard of in the theater. Orchestration is considered an essential part of classical composing, but there are few trained composers on Broadway. Many of its "composers" cannot even notate, let alone write an orchestration; instead, a small group of orchestrators has done the job for most shows, which is why so many sound alike. Too, show music is not orchestrated until it is "routined," or arranged for performance, and that only happens in rehearsal, when the composer usually has no time, even if he has the ability, to orchestrate. Webber, however, had no intention of allowing his music to be altered by a director or by a choreographer's routining of his

songs, and he certainly was not going to let an orchestrator put the final sound to it. He intended it to be performed as he decided and would in the future at least co-orchestrate every show (*Evita* with Hershy Kay and most of the others with David Cullen).

But after *Jesus Christ Superstar* was written, he and Rice could not even find a producer willing to present it, and so they turned to the record companies. The album of *Joseph and the Amazing Technicolor Dreamcoat* had sold well, and with the vast success in 1969 of the so-called "rock opera" *Tommy* by The Who, record companies were even more interested in such pieces. But, Rice later insisted, "our real influence wasn't *Tommy*. It was *Hair.*" The 1967 rock musical had been a great success, but it had little effect on Broadway because producers and composers held their traditional music supreme and lorded their noble line of lyric writing over the crudity of rock-and-roll's language. Of course this only discouraged younger composers and lyricists from ever developing their crafts.

"There is a feeling in the States," Rice said, "that if you're going to do a Broadway show, it should sound like a Broadway show, not a contemporary show. Andrew and I have the advantage of not being caught up in that. We've benefited by not having any tradition to follow. Whatever you may think of *Jesus Christ Superstar*, it was not written with Broadway [sounds] in mind."

Then again, it wasn't yet on Broadway. The fledgling team had reversed the usual process by making an original-cast album before there was an original-cast production. It was only after the record became a hit that there was any interest in staging *Jesus Christ Superstar*. Then, even Harold Prince offered to produce and direct the show, but the Australian entrepreneur Robert Stigwood was quicker at obtaining the rights.

Stigwood's 1971 Broadway production was so overblown that the authors tried to close it down. "The glitz was imposed on us," Rice said. "This show should be small, maybe rough, even violent, but stark. It is not a spectacle." Perhaps, but the complaint about spectacle was going to haunt the team of fledglings. Webber and Rice would insist that it was an unfair criticism and that they had never sought epic size, but they did not seem to realize how big their show ideas were, how big their musical style was, and how big, even operatic, Webber's "through-composing"—the singing of every word—made the shows seem. Too, size of idea was a major reason for their popularity, this willingness to go for broke. Broadway musicals had become cool and tight under the Sondheim influence, but musicals were a lusty medium. Audiences went to them primed for laughter, emotion, and cheering, and these two Englishmen were up for that. There was also something operatic not only about the constant singing but the melodrama, so, in giving Webber and Rice big productions, directors were simply reacting to these stimuli.

Jesus Christ Superstar did not electrify Broadway, although it ran a respectable two years. What followed, however, was extraordinary—in Webber's phrase, "a complete chapter of accidents," for the show sprouted up in a series of concert versions around America, many of them unlicensed. It played to large and enthusiastic audiences. Young people who had no interest in old-fashioned musical theater came to see what they perceived as a rock concert of a favorite album. And so Webber and Rice were attracting the youthful audiences Broadway had ignored and lost.

Like most creative people, Andrew Lloyd Webber is his own harshest and most knowing critic. His one failure, *Jeeves*, was an attempt at a traditional musical comedy. He dismissed it as "kind of a bad version of *Lady Be Good!*" (the 1930s Gershwin show). *Jeeves* starred David Hemmings and Gabriella Drake.

Rock-and-roll remained Rice's enthusiasm, but Webber was already outgrowing it. He convinced Rice to join him on *Jeeves*, a conventional ("book") musical, based on a popular series of novels by P. G. Wodehouse. However, in the midst of writing it, Rice was diverted by an inspiration to create a musical about Eva Perón, the wife and power behind the Argentinean dictator Juan Perón. Webber listened as his friend enthusiastically speculated about what such a show might be like. There had been a miner's strike that had virtually paralyzed England, with "crowds in the streets," Webber recalled. "Things were getting pretty ugly and we found, we thought, a kind of parallel in the story of Eva Perón. We were looking for something that was a cautionary tale about how a liberal democracy is a very fragile flower and can be overturned by an extremist." Perhaps that was fascinating to Webber, but Rice had been inspired by Eva Perón's sexuality. "She was extremely attractive," Webber admitted. But, he rationalized, "she got herself dolled up to please the crowds. We decided to make the show about the two sides of this woman," or so he said. To many observers, *Evita* made more of her sexiness and less of her fascism. The fascistic side was to be underlined for the American version of the show, after much criticism about its glamorization of a dictator.

Rice was so excited about writing *Evita* that he plunged into research for it, leaving Webber to find another collaborator for *Jeeves*. He found the immensely popular British playwright Alan Ayckbourne.

Jeeves's music was conventionally "Broadway," and the numbers came at the end of every scene. "It was kind of a bad version of *Lady Be Good!*" the composer would later say, and it received scathing reviews. But after the premiere, no less than Richard Rodgers called with praise and consolation—which was remarkable, as Rodgers was not prone to appreciate other living composers.

Webber found another source of encouragement in Harold Prince, who sent a note ascribing the failure to the show's *appearance*. "You can't hear a musical if you can't look at it," the particularly visual Prince said, "and *Jeeves* is so ugly, but don't be discouraged. Bank the score."

Webber realized then that "the first thing an audience reacts to is the staging, and Hal's point was, it didn't have to look expensive but it had to look *right*."

He resolved never again to rely on a librettist. If the story or structure was the most important element in a musical, then he was going to control that by telling the story through his songs. "I've never, except for my disaster with *Jeeves*, been involved with anything where there's been significant dialogue," he would later say. "Through-composing allows me to be in the driver's seat."

Work is always the best therapy for failed work, and *Evita* became Webber's preoccupation as it was already Rice's. Their approach was Brechtian, the characters stylized and puppetlike rather than naturalistic. The story was to be told in hard-edged, cartoon episodes, and a communist-fascist tension was introduced through a one-man Greek chorus in the person of Che Guevara. Although Fidel Castro's co-revolutionary had never been involved with Juan and Eva Perón, Webber and Rice took this liberty and used Guevara as a symbol of righteous revolution. At the same time, Guevara could comment to the audience in Brechtian asides.

Webber abandoned the Broadway style of music that he had attempted in *Jeeves* and returned to the kind that had begun to emerge in *Jesus Christ Superstar*. The

Above, and overleaf: Harold Prince's ingenious staging gave *Evita* the impression of being a lavish political spectacle even though the physical production was, in fact, quite spare. The show was one of the most dazzlingly staged of its time. Prince's full-stage presentations in *Evita* helped to communicate a powerful sense of the Peróns' demagoguery.

Cats director Trevor Nunn works with choreographer Gillian Lynne.

team's creative process had settled into a system. Rice would outline the plot, and then the composer would write two-and-a-half hours of music. In the case of *Evita*, it was a blend of ariose Spanish love songs, theatrics, and rock rhythms, much of this symphonically orchestrated, the melodies often juxtaposed against dissonant accompaniments. The words came last. "I try to impose the order on the libretto," Webber says, "by choosing the scenes and the sequence of scenes that I want to set musically."

In making the composer the central figure in the creative process, he was challenging concept musicals — the director-dominated trend of the 1970s — yet soon he would be working with one of the directors in the vanguard of that movement, Harold Prince.

Before that happened, however, *Evita* had to be completed. Tim Rice felt that in writing the libretto, his craftsmanship was also developing. He was, after all, writing an entirely sung libretto. Even the most casual conversations were set to music. While that had been done in grand opera and to some extent in the operettas of Gilbert and Sullivan, there were no precedents in musical theater except for *Porgy and Bess.* With the composer in the dominant position, however, the libretto tended to get short shrift. *Evita*'s lyrics are not always stylish, poetic, or even craftsmanlike, and the sung dialogue is sometimes embarrassing.

Meantime, Webber was seeking an alternative to the usual drone of operatic recitative. So, as if the librettist hadn't headaches enough, Rice had to find a way to set the dialogue to Webber's musical experiments.

They decided at the outset to begin the show in a Buenos Aires movie theater when the projector abruptly shut down and the audience is informed that Eva Perón has died. As the story flashes back, the production takes its cue from this opening, with films and slide projections used throughout. When a rough draft was finished, Webber wired the news to Harold Prince, but at the same time he and Rice jealously guarded their contract to record the work before it was produced on the stage. It was protection against an overly creative director. Once the entire show was etched in vinyl, and known from first word to last, they figured, there would be little room for a director to edit or embroider. As Prince invited Webber to visit his home on the island of Majorca and play the score, the recording was being prepared.

Even at that point, Rice had doubts about the "through-writing," the continuous music, that was so crucial to his partner. "It's very hard to get [the story] over," he felt, "when they're singing everything. With *Jesus Christ Superstar* you could get away with people singing their dialogue because it is such a fantastical story, almost surreal. In *Evita*, because the characters are made larger than life, that is also true to some extent." But while *Evita* opened to great success in London and then in New York, Rice wondered about future projects being sung first-to-last. Meantime, the restless Webber distracted himself with a nontheatrical project: setting to music T. S. Eliot's 1939 cycle of poems, *Old Possum's Book of Practical Cats.*

"Andrew loved those poems since he was a child," Rice remembered, "and he wanted the challenge of setting to music something that was already written and unchangeable." The musicalizing of Eliot's work was first intended as a concert piece for children, but Webber's stage impulse was instinctual. On first hearing his musical settings, Eliot's widow, Valerie, produced a letter in which her husband wrote that *Old Possum's Book of Practical Cats* should end in an occasion about dance. Webber glanced up at Mrs. Eliot and said, "What you've just given me is the difference between what could be just done in a school for children and a musical.

"Let's go for it!"

And so they did. *Practical Cats* (as it was first called) became a choreograhic show, which meant facing up to another negative assumption about the British, namely, that they could not do jazz dancing (as theater choreography is usually called). The idea was to couple this one-act dance show with *Tell Me on a Sunday*, a one-character Webber musical that had already been produced on British television.

The composer had decided to emulate his idol Richard Rodgers and become his own producer. He organized the Really Useful Theatre Company for this purpose, but he still needed a professional producer and found one in Cameron Mackintosh. Webber hoped that Harold Prince, who had done so magnificent a job staging *Evita*, would also direct *Cats*, but the show was too fanciful for him. Prince is a stage intellectual, and his striking visions are directly related to his shows' subjects, to what he calls "metaphoric umbrellas." He is not sympathetic to pure fancy, whether it is the scare show of *Sweeney Todd* or, in the case of Webber's project, anthropomorphic felines. When Webber told him about *Cats*, Prince asked, "Is it a metaphor? Is one of these cats Disraeli? Gladstone? Queen Victoria? Is this about British politics?"

Webber's response was a grin. "Hal," he whispered with affectionate condescension. "It's about *cats*."

Webber and Cameron Mackintosh seemed the only ones who had faith in such an idea. When they tried it out in a six-song version at the composer's private summer theater in Sydmonton, Valerie Eliot supported their approach, but director Trevor Nunn said, "Here I am having a chance with Andrew Lloyd Webber and I'm given the one bum idea he's had."

But Mackintosh and Webber ultimately sold Nunn on the project, and so the artistic director of the Royal Shakespeare Company agreed to direct a commercial project for the first time in his career (doubtless spurred by the Broadway success of his *Nicholas Nickleby* with the RSC). Thus he set to work on a musical that had no script but was only a series of poems set to music. In something of an understatement, Webber remarks, "You can't say *Cats* is a musical in the conventional sense. It has no book nor any story line. It is a theatrical event."

That it was aimed at Broadway from the outset cannot be doubted. "A show doesn't open," Webber said, "until it opens on Broadway." Like so many young people in the British theater, he was just crazy about Broadway musicals.

Even before Trevor Nunn had joined the project, Webber devised a general structure for the show, rearranging the sequence of Eliot's poems. Were this order changed, he later said, putting "Macavity: The Mystery Cat" before "Skimbleshanks," or "Of the Awefull Battle of the Pekes and Pollicles" before "Grizabella: The Glamour Cat," then "the thing just wouldn't work."

When he and Nunn ran out of material in *Old Possum's Book of Practical Cats*, other Eliot poems were brought in, and later, both Nunn and lyricist Richard Stilgoe would add words of their own.

"There was going to be a ghastly moment," Webber said before *Cats* opened, "when a human being came on stage as a cat." Here, Timothy Scott embodies "Mr. Mistoffelees."

Cats proved that the British could make dance musicals after all.

Opposite:
Andrea McArdle *(right)* as a youngster had created the title role of *Annie*. *Starlight Express* took her far from such humble beginnings. McArdle had to escape her identification with *Annie* if she was going to have a career as an adult actress. The robotic toyland of *Starlight Express* did just that.

The roller-skating in *Starlight Express*, while displaying the versatility of Broadway performers, made the cast as accident-prone as a football team.

Opposite:
Michael Crawford originated the role of the Phantom in London, recreated it on Broadway, and then took it to Los Angeles.

With *Cats*, the charge of "spectacle" escalated. "*Evita* is not a spectacle," Webber insisted. "It is merely well staged, and *Jesus Christ Superstar* was supposed to be simple. With *Cats*," he conceded, "well, the spectacle overtook it on Broadway."

Spectacle or not, the likes of this musical had never before been seen, and that was evident from its opening theme, a whimsically eerie fugue performed on a sound synthesizer. This was to be an evening of actors costumed and made up as cats, moving like cats, singing as cats, running through the theater as cats, and Webber felt that the audience had to accept that immediately. He used his control of the orchestrations to support the conceit. "I had to come up with something out of the ordinary," he said, "for there was going to be a ghastly moment when a human being came on stage as a cat. The orchestration was very much a part of that beginning, of how we could make people believe that. We needed to give a sense of danger and unreality at the start." That was the reason for the synthesizer and the eerie fugue. From that point onward, director Nunn and choreographer Gillian Lynne collaborated to make the show a work of dance theater. It spilled into the audience as the cats slithered down the walls, along balcony ledges, and up, down, and across the aisles. It wasn't the first plotless musical. Bob Fosse's *Dancin'* had neither story nor dialogue; revues such as the *Ziegfeld Follies* comprised songs and sketches. But *Cats* was unique in achieving a sense of structure without a story, and despite mixed reviews in London and New York, its success was gigantic in both places. Once again, Webber had touched a responsive audience nerve, and if the critics did not understand him, theatergoers did. As the 1990s began, the show was entering its seventh year on Broadway, a success duplicated the world over, from Moscow to Tokyo and Sydney. It had become the most profitable musical in history, and its advertising slogan seemed almost reasonable — "*Cats*, Now and Forever."

The show made Andrew Lloyd Webber the titan of musical theater. Not even Richard Rodgers and Oscar Hammerstein had put together such consecutive blockbusters as *Evita* and *Cats*. Of course, stage economics had changed. Production costs for a Broadway musical were passing the $4 million mark. Ticket prices had reached $35. It was difficult to compare such amounts with the 1943 profits for *Oklahoma!* or the 1956 profits for *My Fair Lady*. Also, in those years a Broadway musical could not become a worldwide phenomenon as it now could. Perhaps the theater remained a cottage industry in a computer age and perhaps it would always be an anachronism, but Webber's shows took things at least a step toward modern economic reality.

He now could do no wrong. Even *Joseph and the Amazing Technicolor Dreamcoat* was given a Broadway production. "There was never any intention of doing it in the theater," Webber said. "I'd intended only to entertain children," but his youthful effort ran 747 performances. Then *Tell Me on a Sunday*, instead of being paired up with *Cats*, was coupled with a dance piece set to his variations on a Paganini theme. Presented together as *Song and Dance*, it was not a world-class hit but it did run a respectable 436 performances on Broadway. Yet another show Webber had meant for children was tried out in a little church on the vast estate he had bought in Sydmonton, England. "It was at its most effective in that workshop" was Webber's plaint after the little show about animated trains became *Starlight Express*, a technological juggernaut with cantilevered bridges, sleek ramps, and actors whizzing around the theater on roller skates, behind the audience and up along the balconies. Director Trevor Nunn "is very involved with street theater," Webber explained, "and he wanted to

encourage people to come into the theater in a completely different way." But it was the composer who was blamed for yet another extravaganza. "It's my least favorite score," he sadly concluded, adding, "the show never got to my intention."

When *Starlight Express* was exported from London to New York, Webber hoped it would be simplified, but producers had come to associate him with immense profits and wanted lavish sets to justify even higher ticket prices. The show, flashier than ever, became Broadway's first eight-million-dollar musical.

If his great success and such circumstances had made Andrew Lloyd Webber a subject of controversy, these relevant, irrelevant, fortunate, and unfortunate aspects of his career were about to resolve and climax in the most expensive, spectacular, but also artistic musical of them all.

The Phantom of the Opera would seem an inevitable Webber project, a musical about the opera. As an opinionated man with a literary sensibility, he did not admire the 1911 Gaston Leroux novel on which the various film versions had been based, a novel he considered "a mishmash of ideas that Leroux did not really think through to a conclusion." Nor had Webber much patience with the potboiler's various movie

Composer Webber believes that had Christine followed her heart, she would have stayed with the Phantom.

Opposite:
In the spectacular "Masquerade" of *The Phantom of the Opera*, the theme of masks and disguises fills the stage.

69

Andrew Lloyd Webber was as attracted by the operatic background of *Phantom* as he was by its love story.

Putting on the Phantom's face is a two-hour job. The face, basically a foam latex mask, is actually glued to the actor's skin, then touched up with makeup.

versions. What he did like was the melodramatic story, its operatic setting, and, as he put it, "the big emotions. If it hadn't been for that face," he said of the masked composer, "what might have been?" Webber had his own answer. "He was trying to express himself, particularly to a girl, through music," and there was at least some of Andrew Lloyd Webber's personal psychology in this. The phantom, after all, is a composer whose music is derided and who himself vacillates between arrogance and insecurity.

The show's libretto was to have been written by Alan Jay Lerner, but the brilliant author of *My Fair Lady* was already mortally ill when work was to begin. What *The Phantom of the Opera* might have been with a Lerner libretto only stirs the imagination. The ultimate text, by Charles Hart and Richard Stilgoe, is seldom more than adequate and is sometimes, frankly, banal. It starts out with more spoken dialogue than any Andrew Lloyd Webber musical since *Jeeves*. We are at an auction of relics at the Paris Opera House and as the famous old chandelier of the place is put on the block, the legend of the Phantom is recounted, the legend of a masked composer living in the bowels of the opera house and haunting the place. Webber feels that this expository material had to be gotten out of the way and that it would never have been clear had it been sung. Ironically, the show could have managed perfectly well without it.

The Phantom of the Opera really begins when accidents such as falling scenery begin to happen backstage during rehearsals and the company sings

He's here
The Phantom of the Opera
He is with us...
It's the ghost...

A beautiful, young singer in the chorus, Christine Daaé, has been heard by the Phantom and he has fallen in love with her (and her voice), almost identifying with her.

> I am your Angel of Music
> Come to me: Angel of Music

Beneath his spell, she comes to his lair in the labyrinth under the opera house. What Broadway musical has dared to be so outrageously romantic? The librettists only take their cue from the rapturous composer.

> I have brought you
> to the seat of sweet
> music's throne . . .
> to this kingdom
> where all must pay
> homage to music

And who is he?

> this loathsome gargoyle, who
> burns in hell, but secretly
> yearns for heaven

He is a familiar figure, the gentle monster tamed by a loving woman as in *Beauty and the Beast*, *Frankenstein*, *King Kong*, and *Of Mice and Men*.

After much spooking of rehearsals, and razzing of the diva for her singing and the tenor for his girth, the Phantom begins to make threats on behalf of Christine Daaé—that she should replace the diva:

> So it is to be war between us! If these demands are not met a disaster beyond your imagination will occur!

After repeated threats and more accidents, culminating with the famous (and unconvincing) crash of the real theater's chandelier before intermission, the Phantom now insists that his own opera, *Don Juan Triumphant*, be performed with Christine in the lead. Surely, this exultantly dissonant opera (no Puccini here) was Webber's most personal musical statement thus far and, perhaps as well, his finest and most exciting music. It is difficult to think of a contemporary stage composer other than Leonard Bernstein who might have composed it.

At the same time, and this is the nub of it, such songs as "The Music of the Night," "The Point of No Return," "Think of Me," and "All I Ask of You" are so rich and soaring as to belong in the grandest of Broadway traditions, that of Jerome Kern and Richard Rodgers.

Yet Webber is more than a melodist. With *Phantom* he perfected an ingenious way of using parts of his songs for the sung conversations, replacing the traditional drone of recitative with musical phrases from songs already sung or yet to be sung. By weaving these musical phrases throughout the sung conversations, he creates a continuity. A novel technique, instead of being recognized as such, it was criticized as repetitious.

Christine ultimately rejects the Phantom for a handsome young lover, and in a heartbreaking denouement, the wretched masked composer sacrifices his revenge to set the couple free. Webber, dramatist that he is, reveled in this martyred romance, but in something of a personal revelation he later said, "We all know that Christine wants to remain with the Phantom and would do that if she could."

The show is plainly an excuse to enjoy and indulge his love of opera. While the excerpts of "operas" are presumably the work of fictitious composers, Webber's knowledgeable parodies of Gounod, Handel, and Meyerbeer are cheerfully bitchy, and he proudly describes his "Prima Donna" ensemble as using "every operatic reference you could find."

He also believes that the show "has taken things along the road that I believe musical theater just *has* to go, which is toward the total kind of experience. . . that can envelop you within music."

The Phantom of the Opera certainly does take Webber's theory down that road, and while it is not yet a smooth road, it is neither meandering nor misleading. The all-sung, or through-composed, musical is only the latest in a series of approaches taken by various men of the musical theater toward a continuously musical musical. Oscar Hammerstein's approach, since followed by Stephen Sondheim, was to interweave music and lyrics with dialogue. George Gershwin's in *Of Thee I Sing* and *Let 'Em Eat Cake* was to have dialogue sung in the style of Gilbert and Sullivan. In *Street Scene*, Kurt Weill sought to make the Broadway musical "a real blending of drama and music in which the singing continues naturally where the speaking stops and the spoken word as well as the dramatic action are embedded in overall musical structure."

Composers have not been alone in seeking a thoroughly musical theater. As they (naturally) sought the solution in music, directors have looked for it in continuous musical staging. Webber's setting of every word to music does indeed make a story hard to follow. It does discourage sophisticated librettos (as, for that matter, do concept musicals with their minimized dialogue). His through-composing also requires the singing of all conversation, which, when someone sings for a cup of coffee, can sound foolish and blur the important distinction between dialogue and lyrics. Song lyrics, after all, use poetic devices such as rhyme, metaphor, meter, theme, and symbol in an effort to orchestrate an idea. When a lyric is not complete unto itself but is fragmented into dialogue, it is no longer structured and does not serve as the connection between dialogue and music that is a lyric's crucial function.

Webber's entirely sung shows, then, are not the ultimate solution to the quest for continuously musical theater. But neither is the concept musical. All of these developments, however, do converge toward that goal.

It is exhilarating that Andrew Lloyd Webber has not only joined in this exciting artistic search but in the process has the resounding approval of audiences. Nothing is so special to Broadway as the show that blends artistry with popularity. Of such are the most tremendous of hits made, from *Oklahoma!* to *Guys and Dolls*, *My Fair Lady*, *Fiddler on the Roof*, *A Chorus Line*, *Evita*, and *The Phantom of the Opera*.

With *Phantom* established as a huge hit, Webber set about responding to accusations that he wrote spectacles only. "Both of us," he said, speaking for Trevor Nunn, who had been equally blamed for overproducing not only *Cats* but *Starlight*

In the convoluted plot of *Aspects of Love*, Alex begins as the adolescent in love with the older actress, Rose, and ends as the older man whom her adolescent daughter loves.

Express, "badly wanted to do something on a smaller scale." The smaller musical that Webber had in mind was one he had been considering even before *The Phantom of the Opera*. It was a chamber-sized musical to reunite the team of Webber and Rice, which would be based on a novella called *Aspects of Love*, written in 1955 by David Garnett, a minor member of London's Bloomsbury Group. Webber had already begun work on this show when Rice was distracted by another project *(Chess)*, and so *Phantom* came first, using some of the *Aspects of Love* material. Now the smaller musical was again postponed, this time because of an invitation from Prince Edward for Webber and Rice to write a brief original musical in celebration of Queen Elizabeth's sixtieth and Prince Philip's sixty-fifth birthdays. Such requests are a nice thing about being royal. The birthday present became *Cricket*, a half-hour show presented at Windsor Castle in the summer of 1986 under Nunn's direction. There were ten new songs in it and, given the Webber-Rice reputation, commercial offers presented themselves immediately. ("Perhaps we could have gotten four shows a day out of it," the whimsical Rice said.) But *Cricket* was to be performed only once more, although several of its melodies would subsequently find their way into *Aspects of Love*.

Work on that show finally began, but without Rice, following the perhaps inevitable re-falling out. *Aspects* can best be described as sophisticatedly eclectic, part *La Ronde* (Anatole Schnitzler), part *Les Liaisons Dangereuses* (Charderos de Lacios), and part *Smiles of a Summer Night* (Ingmar Bergman). Of course the latter was the basis for the Harold Prince–Stephen Sondheim musical *A Little Night Music*. Comparisons with that show are inevitable, and it could well seem as if Webber was confronting Sondheim to decide who has the greater public appeal.

In Webber's show (set, like Sondheim's, on a country estate), the songs are as rich and diverse as ever, from the overriding "Love Changes Everything" to the haunting ballad "Seeing Is Believing," the emotional "First Man You Remember," and the impassioned "Anything but Lonely." In the story, a seventeen-year-old Englishman falls in love with an older actress and brings her to his uncle's country estate for a week of romance. When the sophisticated uncle arrives, the actress transfers her affections, and thus begins a tale of intertwining romances and unfaithful lovers in various combinations of sex, age, and betrayals.

Webber hoped for an elegant script along the lines of Da Ponte's for *The Marriage of Figaro*, although he hardly had reason to expect such writing from inexperienced librettists — Don Black and Charles Hart. It is tempting to theorize that the composer did not really want strong collaborators.

Perhaps inevitably, the critical onslaught awaiting *Aspects of Love* in New York was the nastiest of all. This was revenge for the successes of *Evita*, *Cats*, *The Phantom of the Opera*, and even *Starlight Express* despite bad reviews. *Aspects of Love* deserved better treatment. It presented Webber as a confident melodist, formidable in his control of the popular operatic musical he had developed. It demonstrated that he could be intimate in his theatrics. It showed that his kind of theater, entirely sung and in a contemporary musical vernacular, was adaptable to various subjects and moods. But despite a run of 377 performances, it became the biggest financial loser ($11 million) in Broadway history. Probably nobody knew better than Webber himself that however he wished to dominate the creative process, music could never come first in the theater. The book is the most important element, always the book.

So he had to face up to the issue that has frustrated every major artist in Broadway musicals — that of collaboration. It is an infuriating situation for a creative genius, and Broadway's best have dealt with it variously. Some have self-destructed with compromise. Some have fled. The future of Andrew Lloyd Webber would depend on how he approached it, for plainly, now, he needed writer-collaborators who were not inferiors but equals. Were he to accept them and work with them as equals his domination of the musical theater could very well lead to the great breakthrough that all have been seeking, which is the thing unto itself, an absolutely musical theater.

A static, symmetrical staging marks the climactic match in *Chess.*

Overleaf:
In an emotional peak from *Aspects of Love,* a daughter dances for her father. Audiences invariably break into applause in the midst of this song, "The First Man You Remember," and that is the product of a Broadway musical in high gear.

4
HAROLD
PRINCE

*"You've got to think of it as
the American musical,
not the Broadway musical."*

The team for *Merrily We Roll Along* had frequently worked together: from the left are choreographer Ron Field, associate producer Ruth Mitchell, director Harold Prince, and, in the background, composer Stephen Sondheim.

There is a tradition underlying Broadway musicals, the style and feel and rhythm, that has made them the specially loved stage animals they are. At its best, this tradition has provided for an American stage greatness and nobody in the modern American musical theater personifies it more fully than Harold Prince. Indeed, in this producer-director can be seen the past, present, and future of Broadway musicals. He uniquely blends the two contradictory and yet mutually stimulating aspects of Broadway—its commercial and artistic natures.

One might never have anticipated anything resembling creative greatness from the youthful Prince, who began his career as a would-be producer by working as a stage manager. Educated to be a businessman, business was his metier, and his first chance at show business came in 1954, when (at the age of 26) he co-produced *The Pajama Game.* What followed was a series of successful and stylish musicals involving the finest talents on Broadway—such choreographers as Jerome Robbins and Bob Fosse, and composers like Leonard Bernstein, Stephen Sondheim, Jerry Bock and Sheldon Harnick, Richard Adler and Jerry Ross, Lee Adams and Charles Strouse, John Kander and Fred Ebb. But the key figure in Prince's future, oddly enough, was the first, least artistic, but most practical of his creative allies—George Abbott.

The legendary "Mister Abbott" was the reigning director of Broadway musicals when Prince started out producing *The Pajama Game.* Abbott directed other early Prince hits, including *Damn Yankees* and *Fiorello!*, but perhaps more important, he trained the future leaders of our musical theater, Robbins and Fosse and Prince himself. It was from Abbott that Prince learned the fundamentals of stage directing—the "traffic management," as he calls the movement of scenery and actors. In short, he learned to be clear-eyed, logical, and pragmatic, as Abbott was, while absorbing notions of artistry and aspiration from Jerome Robbins.

The Harold Prince of 1958 could hardly have imagined himself a future director as he publicly complained about being lampooned as a pushy and impertinent young producer in *Say, Darling*, a satire of the making of *The Pajama Game*. But soon enough (1963) he would himself be directing *She Loves Me*, an elegant chamber musical that would ultimately endure while other flashier and more immediately successful shows did not.

Prince was developing a reputation as Broadway's classiest producer, not as publicized as David Merrick, but perhaps even more successful. Indeed, the Prince imprimateur had come to be so consistently associated with profitable shows that he dispensed with traditional backers' auditions and was able to raise the capital he needed simply by notifying his family of investors that a new musical was being readied. And with such shows as *West Side Story* and *Fiddler on the Roof*, how could his backers complain?

Years later, with the 1970s drawing to a close, Prince would have almost completely abandoned producing. The cost of it had grown too great, and its responsibilities were less rewarding than those of directing. When Jerome Robbins retired to the ballet after *Fiddler on the Roof*, Prince assumed the great choreographer-director's artistic mantle, even his beard, and so the frenetic young businessman was transformed into a craftsmanly director — an unusually well-educated and especially painterly one. The callow bourgeois who had been caricatured in *Say, Darling* was now a handsome, tweedy, educated, earnest, and articulate leader of the most exciting new development on Broadway, the "concept musical," and Prince led this movement in collaboration with Stephen Sondheim. Forming a new kind of team, the producer-director and composer-lyricist, they created a series of artworks for the commercial theater — *Company, Follies, A Little Night Music, Pacific Overtures.*

The concept musical was born of a need sensed almost from the start of musical-making — to make musicals different from plays, to make them something of their own kind, continuously musical and yet not operatic.

West Side Story could be considered the breakthrough show for this genre, with its unusually extensive choreography and its propulsively rhythmic movement, even during sequences that are not actual dance numbers. Jerome Robbins expanded this approach when he directed *Fiddler on the Roof*. Prince then continued the development in *Cabaret*, but since he was not himself a choreographer, he extended the show's staging concept beyond actual dance to its very appearance. During the cabaret sequences of the show, dialogue, song, dance, and movement flowed integrally within an overall picture that transformed *Cabaret* into a theatrical painting inspired by Georg Grosz, the master German Expressionist.

Overleaf:
The graphics and stage pictures of Grind created a marvelous sense of period, mood, and milieu.

The subsequent collaborations with Sondheim had each show building upon the developments of the prior one, as *Company, Follies, A Little Night Music*, and *Pacific Overtures* in turn strengthened the libretto, the choreography, the musical dialogue, and the visual aspects of such thematic musicals. Unlike the traditional "book musicals," these were, from the outset, based on production *concepts* that — in Prince's mind, at least — were related to themes. For as an intellectual, he could not be interested in a show without a point. And he would find a visual notion for that "metaphoric umbrella" under which the show would spread.

Written as a rock opera for records, *Evita* was ostensibly finished when Webber and Rice brought it to Prince, but the director was still able to exercise considerable creativity. This scene, for instance, was his idea — the metaphoric game of musical chairs played by Juan Perón and his military colleagues for political power. Prince also used film clips to lend *Evita* a sense of documentary reality. It was a rare example of multimedia production devices actually working on Broadway.

Perhaps Prince and Sondheim needed a break from each other after a decade of nearly exclusive collaboration. Sondheim is an uncompromising artist who not only follows his own inspiration but sometimes even seems to seek the unpopular. Prince, while certainly idealistic, has never forgotten the lessons in pragmatism learned at the feet of George Abbott. He understood and accepted the commercial basis for all Broadway theater. In 1977 he made a pivotal decision — one that affected in a very serious way his own future, Sondheim's, Andrew Lloyd Webber's, and the Broadway musical's. He went to London to direct *Evita*, and his staging of the Webber and Rice show must be considered a landmark for all of these reasons. This magnificent production established Harold Prince internationally and made Andrew Lloyd Webber the chief rival of Prince's longtime friend and collaborator Sondheim, forming a professional triangle between the two composers (who, curiously, share the same birthday, March 22) and the director, one that would be superimposed upon the musical theater's immediate future and perhaps determine its form in the long run.

In 1979, as if to do for Sondheim what he'd done for Webber, Prince gave a similar size, if not electricity, to *Sweeney Todd, the Demon Barber of Fleet Street.* Sondheim would come to consider this an overproduction but when *Evita* was itself produced on Broadway, its British success was duplicated.

Then Prince's well ran dry. He staged a series of disasters, the first *(Merrily We Roll Along)* apparently wearing out the collaborative history with Sondheim. The composer moved on to other directors, while some on Broadway, long resentful of Prince's confidence (some said arrogance), were already pronouncing him, as it was cruelly put, dead in the business.

When he resurfaced after a year of catching his breath from these jolts *(A Doll's Life, Grind)* while staging operas around the world, it was with the conviction that it was not he who had died but the business itself, Broadway's commercial system. The American theater had to be decentralized, he believed, because its economics discouraged artistic or experimental shows. By that Prince meant not the avant-garde but unusual shows, like *West Side Story, Fiddler on the Roof,* and *Company.* He was convinced that Broadway had become a center of safe mass-market entertainment. Anything ambitious would have to be created and established elsewhere. Only then would it have the cachet and advance publicity necessary to survive in New York.

"Elsewhere" included London, which Prince enjoyed "because [they have] a healthy theater there. Everything doesn't have to be a hit. Shows run." In 1986, he went there to direct another Andrew Lloyd Webber show, the stupendously successful *Phantom of the Opera,* and when that success was repeated in New York, the Harold Prince roller coaster of good times and bad cascaded to a triumphant crest. He had survived. "*Evita* and *Phantom,*" Webber would himself say, "are the two productions of my work that have been closest to my intentions." They were among the most fabulous successes in Broadway history and were also among its most creative and magnificent productions. Harold Prince's decade had truly mirrored the ups and downs of the musical stage.

Choreographer Larry Fuller shows Patti LuPone a step or two for *Evita.*

When Andrew Lloyd Webber visited the Prince vacation home on the Balearic island of Majorca to audition *Evita* in 1977, the director responded with enthusiasm. His reservations were minor, but he warned the young composer that he had already agreed to direct another show *(On the Twentieth Century).* "If you're willing to wait," he said, "then I'll commit to *Evita* next," and Webber was certainly willing to wait for the man responsible for producing and/or directing some of Broadway's greatest musicals.

And so in this seemingly orderly way, the development of Broadway musicals continued. For Harold Prince was a link between present and past. Indeed, he had become a mentor himself, training Michael Bennett by engaging him as the choreographer for *Company* and co-director for *Follies.* And, between the shows he had produced and those he'd directed, he represented Broadway fundamentals, Broadway professionalism, and Broadway possibilities, encompassing its commercial as well as artistic natures. He was now about to extend this sphere of influence to Andrew Lloyd Webber.

Working with the hypersensitive Englishman was a delicate business. Prince would express his opinions paternally. "Andrew," he would say gently, "you're a dramatic composer. You can do better than that," and the psychology would work. "I would respond like a child to a parent," the composer recalled, "apologizing and feeling as if I had done my homework badly."

Much as Webber disliked choreography, and much as Prince himself avoided dance, he urged if not outright dancing, more writing for musical staging, so that as an entirely sung musical, *Evita* would have some relief from vocalism. Prince knew that even a silent scene could convey information — sometimes more effectively than with words. For instance, in depicting Juan Perón's climb to power, Prince suggested that five generals play musical chairs — on rocking chairs. Webber and Tim Rice took this idea and wrote "The Art of the Possible." This stylized scene of one general after another being removed became one of the most striking in *Evita*.

A Doll's Life was a misconceived show, but its stage pictures were ravishing.

Below:
Grind proved to be one of Prince's most frustrating experiences. It starred Ben Vereen.

Prince also urged that Eva Perón be shown as she sees Juan for the first time and sets her sights on him. This was to become a vivid scene at a political rally when the ambitious young actress stands backstage, watching Perón address an unseen crowd somewhere beyond the stage wings. His echoing microphone and the roaring responses, hugely amplified, create the impression of massed thousands. As for "Don't Cry for Me, Argentina," Webber decided, "this song was going to be our 'Over the Rainbow.' I had seen Judy Garland sing that in London at the end of her career, drunk, mumbling, and staggering through it so badly that the audience threw pennies at her. That was the notion I had for 'Don't Cry for Me, Argentina.' It was to be an anthem that, at the show's end, finally twisted itself back upon the girl. I talked to Hal a lot about that."

Prince suggested that, instead of Eva simply re-singing this haunting theme, she stand at a floor microphone as if giving a speech. Then a voice would shout, "Sorry! Can't hear you," with a degrading disrespect similar to Garland's treatment, and so the show began to take form even before the recording was made.

When *Evita* opened at the Prince Edward Theatre in London in June of 1978, the record album was already a success, and so the audience was to an extent pre-sold. But *Evita* had been raised to another power onstage. If Webber and Rice's *Jesus Christ Superstar* had appealed as a rock concert of a popular album, *Evita* was pure and absolute *theater*. It had muscle and size without mass. Its visual strength was provided not by lavish sets, but by giant banners and dramatic lighting devices as well as film clips. In these ways, and in one of the greatest demonstrations of musical directing, Prince made a relatively spare production seem immense. Yet, for all the originality and energy of this new, theatrical form of opera, many critics responded negatively, and with moral indignation in the bargain. A dictator was deemed an inappropriate subject for a musical, especially a dictator whose appeal is sexual. Thus, musical theater was up against the old prejudice, the presumption that it was supposed to be featherbrained.

Those who did admire the show tended to credit the directing rather than the materials, and the ever-sensitive Webber interpreted this as, "Well, of course, this eighth-rate musical has only been saved by this American's production." But audiences do not care where the credit lies or whether dictators are sexy, and public approval of the show was explosive. Indeed, the success of *Evita* surpassed that of any British musical in history.

Prince, meantime, returned to Broadway and Sondheim. The team had once been inseparable and unique, dedicated to making Broadway-sized shows of daring and innovation. Though few of their collaborations had turned any profit, financing was still available because of their reputation and prestige, and in 1980, the latest of their works, *Sweeney Todd, the Demon Barber of Fleet Street*, was in the seventh month of what would be an eighteen-month run, holding its own despite a shaky box office.

But Prince, while tactful, did not seem proud of *Sweeney Todd*. "When Steve first talked about it," he said, "at the intermission the audience would be served meat pies, so you can see what the spirit of that show would have been. It was just campy." Prince needed his musicals to be *about* something, and *Sweeney Todd* it seemed was merely about blood. Only when the set designer, Eugene Lee, suggested framing the show within an enormous factory did the director find his "metaphoric umbrella" for it. Prince took the factory setting and, at least in his own mind, related the story to the Industrial Revolution. After that, whenever anyone asked what was made in that factory, he would reply simply, "They make Sweeney Todd," by which he meant that oppressive social conditions can destroy the goodness of the human spirit.

Perhaps it was a rationalization, perhaps this was not really the message in the materials, but it was the rationale the director used to express himself, translating his thoughts into stage pictures.

Sondheim is a notoriously slow worker, but, possibly influenced by *Evita*, he wrote more music for *Sweeney Todd* than he had previously composed for any show. Its dialogue is spoken, not sung, but kept to a minimum, and a huge amount of the music is sung back-and-forth between characters. "The show isn't an opera," Prince insisted even when the New York City Opera revived it. "There's more dialogue in it than in *Evita*." But certainly, the distinctions between musical theater and opera were blurring.

Like most of the Sondheim–Prince shows, *Sweeney Todd* was acclaimed and prized, but like most of those shows too, its appeal was limited. The greater public "wouldn't come," the director said, "because of what it was about."

Merrily We Roll Along was the victim, director Harold Prince said, of an incompletely formed staging concept. Others felt that the cast was too young and inexperienced to play characters who age several generations in the course of the show. The central character here, for instance, Producer Franklin Shepard is supposed to be forty-three years old.

Oddly enough, while *Sweeney Todd* had the look of art, the next Sondheim–Prince musical, *Merrily We Roll Along*, looked much more *Broadway* and yet was more serious. Of course, all art does not have to make a point. Only Harold Prince's. For this show, librettist George Furth (who had written *Company*) adapted an obscure George S. Kaufman–Moss Hart comedy of 1937. Like that original, this libretto tells its story by starting at the end and working backward in time. There seemed no reason for this, and it inevitably confused audiences.

Merrily We Roll Along is about a pair of songwriters who begin as high school idealists and wind up as enemies because one of them becomes a cynic. The story spans some twenty-five years, and Prince decided that instead of hiring older actors to play the characters when young, he would have youthful actors do the aging. This posed a second problem: finding inexperienced young actors who would play older characters convincingly.

Third, and worst, "I could never find a staging concept for it," Prince later admitted. Sondheim and Furth had agreed that the show be done without scenery or costumes, but Broadway tickets were at the (then) fearsome price of $35 and the show's producers hadn't the nerve to give the audience only a show for their money. And so Prince had his designer build a gymnasium with a set of bleachers, "which was very hard to look at," he conceded, "and very grim. Ironically, a totally bare stage would not have been so hard to look at — or grim."

Merrily We Roll Along opened "cold" in New York. Instead of going out of town to try out, it played previews while undergoing revisions. The word was soon traveling along the gossip lines: Sondheim and Prince were launching a bomb. This kind of sniping has long been a regrettable Broadway tradition, as if, in the chancy world of the theater, someone else's failure leaves one fewer setback for the rest. As Sondheim himself said, "It isn't enough for you to be a hit. Everyone else has to fail." And a show that is previewing in New York is available to every nosy backbiter, turning the nasty whispers into a cruel racket.

The din made work difficult, but *Merrily We Roll Along* was probably beyond rescue, and after receiving abusive reviews that even overlooked Sondheim's scintillating score, it ran a humiliating sixteen performances. In the decade ahead, various directors would seek to fix it at various regional theaters, inspired by Sondheim's witty lyrics and exhilarating music, but none of the productions solved the show's problems to the satisfaction of interested producers. Ten years after its Broadway opening, Prince himself said, "I still don't know what it should look like." And so this score, one of Sondheim's most engaging, is likely to remain heard but not seen.

Coincidentally or not, just as the central characters in *Merrily We Roll Along* break up their partnership (and friendship), Prince and Sondheim suspended their collaboration after the show closed. Was Sondheim too idealistic and artistic for a Harold Prince who had been a producer and thus had a sense of commercial reality? Did Prince have a bit of the pragmatic George Abbott in him, believing to some extent that to be good a production should be popular? Did he just miss having hit shows, weary of prestigious failures? Or was it all of the above? Was Prince, in all those ways, a reflection of Broadway, with all its sides, its artistic aspirations and its audience of masses, its greatness and toughness? After the closing of *Merrily We Roll*

When Prince directed Leonard Bernstein's *Candide* for the New York City Opera, he had to restage it as a proscenium presentation. Ironically, a decade earlier he had rescued the show from cult status by replacing its original proscenium version with an arena-style production. *Candide* has since become an opera house staple, like another Broadway musical, *Porgy and Bess.*

Roza proved to Prince that Broadway musicals cannot be small.

Along, he and Sondheim talked like the parents of a lost child. They were the creators of some of Broadway's proudest musicals. "But we both thought," Prince said, "it would be a good idea to take a break from each other for a while. You begin to finish each other's sentences."

He was no longer a producer. He hadn't even exclusively produced *Sweeney Todd* or *Merrily*. Perhaps in past, golden times he had been able to raise money easily, but he considered that no longer possible when the cost of a musical was approaching $5 million. Now, instead of one creative producer supervising a production, groups of investors joined together and produced by committee. Many of these so-called producers were inexperienced, Prince felt. As a result, he said in 1988, "You could not do *West Side Story* anymore. You wouldn't be able to raise the money. *Fiddler on the Roof* would have to be done somewhere else because you could not raise $5 million to do [it]."

Not everyone agreed. Cameron Mackintosh didn't. Was Prince being realistic? Or was he speaking about Broadway-style producing and Broadway-style shows (a style he seemed uniquely to embody)?

Merrily We Roll Along shot Harold Prince into a tunnel of flops. In the fall of 1982 he directed, of all things, a musical sequel to Henrik Ibsen's dour play *A Doll's House,* not an idea to set the heart dancing. The libretto by musical comedy specialists Betty Comden and Adolph Green was a speculation about Nora's life after she slams the door on her husband at the final curtain of Ibsen's play. In all the years since, audiences had not seemed unduly curious about her fate.

With so unlikely, if not altogether hopeless, a premise, and with lyrics also by Comden and Green set to music by the gifted composer Larry Grossman, *A Doll's Life* proved aimless, and certainly unmusical. It closed after five performances.

Prince felt that *A Doll's Life* "had many good things about it, but it was dead wrong for Broadway"—and who knew Broadway better than he? With debacle coming on the heels of disaster, he ran for the cover of opera, where productions did not depend on reviews or box offices. No producers or investors were involved. An opera was not supposed to turn a profit, and the work took him far from Broadway's sudden jolts, around the world where he could learn and escape, and when he came back, it was with a show much more in line with what he'd been doing with Sondheim. This was *Grind,* set on stage and backstage at an old burlesque theater. Prince himself described the show with one of his metaphoric umbrellas: "a revue about violence. Violence so totally integrating itself into our lives that we no longer even notice it; personal violence, marital, political. This was a show where every kind of violence took place—*in the night.*"

To make it a concept musical, then, was his intent and he believed that as a creative director he was shaping a show that, like *Pacific Overtures,* was nonlinear and impressionistic rather than straightforward and naturalistic. *Pacific Overtures* had taken musical librettos to an advanced level. Prince felt that *Grind* was following in the same direction, only to be wrenched out of his hands "by a five-million-dollar budget and eighteen hundred producers—and their wives," making it "not the kind of show I do."

A Doll's Life featured Betsy Joslyn with George Hearn, who was to become one of the leading singer–actors in contemporary musical theater.

Under pressure to hire a star, he agreed to cast Ben Vereen, and thus began the compromises that would make this one of his most bitter stage experiences. *Grind* opened to nasty reviews, his third consecutive set of them. The show eked out a 79-performance run, even that only in hope of winning a Tony Award to stimulate business. Such a hope might have been pathetic, but it was not absurd, so bad were the musical theater times of 1985. There were so few good candidates, in fact, that *Grind* was actually nominated as the Best Musical of the season.

Prince was hardly optimistic about winning, even though the only viable competitor was the painfully unprofessional Huckleberry Finn musical *Big River*. Such a show besting him would be a slap in the face while his pants were down. Small wonder he was in a foul temper backstage at a rehearsal for those Tony Awards; Andrew Lloyd Webber was there as well, to remind him of better times. He invited Prince to join him for a drink after rehearsal, asking him, "What are you up to?"

"I'm just looking for a romantic plot," the director replied, understandably weary of *Grind*'s metaphoric umbrella.

"I've already got it," Webber said. "I'm going to do *The Phantom of the Opera*."

"Partner," Prince grinned, "you're on." And just in time too, for *Big River* did win the Tony Award and *Grind* closed promptly thereafter.

Was ever a musical better staged than *The Phantom of the Opera?* Not likely. Harold Prince's recent experience in opera might have been a preparation prescribed for this opera-devoted musical. The scenes of rehearsals and the operatic satires are drenched in authenticity. In purely visual terms, Prince's stage pictures take musical theater to magical realms, with imagery that is not only strong and beautiful but of a piece with the show's theme of creativity and broken love.

The Phantom of the Opera was the work of a Harold Prince at the peak of his artistic abilities, but it also offered him a way out; it appeared to free him from the need to have his musicals deal with social or political issues. When he told Webber that he was looking for a romantic story, it was as if he needed escape as much as audiences do when they go to the theater. But in *Phantom of the Opera*, Harold Prince found more than escape. He found an involvement with the heart.

For all the showmanship in this glorious musical, for all its fabulous pictures and gorgeous melodies, the inner strength lies in the love story, the old favorite of poets and balladeers.

However, Harold Prince still had to find a musical theater of his own, beyond Andrew Lloyd Webber blockbusters. His reality was Broadway. That was where he had started out as a stage manager, developed as a producer, and blossomed as a director. For better or worse, he was a child of that commercial theater; indeed, he seemed to personify its every phase, from the musical comedy of his mentor George Abbott to the musical theater of Sondheim and the commercial art of Webber.

Now, it seemed to him, the system that had fostered this broad range of musicals was being corrupted by costs, pressures, and circumstances. "The sooner you get musicals being done elsewhere," he said, in rejection of Broadway, "the sooner things will get better." He dreamed of plays that could be developed away

The Kiss of the Spider Woman, starring John Rubinstein and Kevin Gray, had originality and possibilities. Premature reviews did not help develop them.

from investors and critics, away from the instant box office test. He decided that a logical "elsewhere" was a regional theater, like Center Stage in Baltimore.

Naturally, such a theater could not be expected to produce a musical on the Broadway scale. Although smaller shows having one set and a limited cast were being tried in New York, none were succeeding. There had been intimate musicals of style and quality, but they hadn't attracted audiences. Prince thought his *Roza* would. When it didn't, he concluded that small musicals were not the answer. Broadway musicals were big by nature.

He sought out places where big shows of artistic merit could be tested without running the critical gauntlet. He seemed to find that haven in a 1990 project called New Musicals at the Performing Arts Center of the State University of New York at Purchase, in suburban New York. An ambitious notion, New Musicals projected four full-sized, fully designed, fully orchestrated productions each year, written and staged by Broadway professionals. In a relaxed atmosphere they could be seen for what they had and be tinkered with, free of Broadway pressures.

Prince agreed to direct the first of them, *The Kiss of the Spider Woman*, based on the Manuel Puig novel. Its score was written by John Kander and Fred Ebb, the libretto by playwright Terrence McNally. It was a risky notion for a musical, this story of an unlikely pair of convicts in a South American prison, one a political prisoner and the other a particularly effeminate homosexual. Their story is of friendship, humanity, and love, turned musical through the device of a fictitious old Hollywood movie called *The Kiss of the Spider Woman*. As the gay prisoner describes this campy movie to his unreceptive cell-mate, it is glitzily performed in juxtaposition to the grim reality of prison.

When the show opened, it might have been exactly as Prince anticipated, a flawed, chancy, but promising work in progress. It had many problems but it also had wonderful music, moments of power, and unquestionable potential. However, pressures reached out to squelch it. The New York critics brought Broadway the "forty-five minutes" to Purchase, reviewing the show before its time and treating it as if it were a finished work, rejecting and possibly ending it.

Prince had every reason to be furious, and he was. A project designed to rescue Broadway musicals had been sabotaged by critics less interested in the theater's survival than in beating one another to the latest in show business. And yet, perhaps there was something strangely right in all this. Perhaps Prince was being forced to face an unpleasant but basic and enduring truth of Broadway musicals. Perhaps he had been deceiving himself, allowing himself to be as idealistic and insulated as his old friend and collaborator Stephen Sondheim. But Prince had, after all, been a producer. He had grown up on the financial side of Broadway and knew that for better or worse, it was a commercial theater. Whatever had been done there, whatever had been accomplished on Broadway, the great, the entertaining, or the mediocre, had been done by the commercial rules. They are not nice rules, nor rules to be pure by, but they are the rules by which musicals have always been made.

And perhaps future greatness in the musical theater will have to be conceived according to those same rules, just as greatness has been achieved in the past.

5

TOMMY TUNE

Writing about Irving Berlin, composer Alec Wilder, himself the author of such splendid songs as "While We're Young" and "I'll Be Around," confronted the astonishing variety of Berlin's music, the absolute lack of pattern or repetition, the seemingly endless invention of melody, form, and structure, and muttered, "Where does he *get* these things?"

The same might be asked of Tommy Tune. Among all the choreographer-directors, his work is the most diverse, the least predictable, the most fanciful and imaginative. Indeed, inventiveness is the essence of the Tommy Tune career, with himself the best invention, for he seemed to have appeared wholly formed and in working order. He simply arrived, and he was the only choreographer-director to arrive on Broadway during the 1980s.

The timing could not have been better, for the others were disappearing fast. Following Jerome Robbins's semi-retirement, Gower Champion, Michael Bennett, and Bob Fosse died. An entire generation of Broadway choreographer-directors was disappearing, and the loss was not merely of stagers and dance masters but of theater men who had assumed roles as showmakers. Superseding, at the creative center, those who wrote the scripts and composed the songs, these directors had themselves become the authors of musicals. They created through production, with the stage their medium and performance their language. Perhaps it was true that choreographers danced because they couldn't talk, but in the search for a musical theater divorced from drama, a little less talk was in order along with a lot more action. And from these artists of production emerged the stage-constructed concept musicals of the 1970s and 1980s.

But by 1990, only Tommy Tune and Harold Prince remained to pursue this exciting trend, and of course Prince, while unsurpassed at coordinating his work with a choreographer's, still was not one himself. Like the composer-lyricist whose words suit his music better than any partner's might, a director-choreographer can

Tommy Tune emerged fully developed as a director with his very first assignment, Eve Merriam's *The Club*, off-Broadway. His use of white tape would prove typical of a refreshingly antic visual sense.

Overleaf:
Like most Tommy Tune shows, *Nine* capitalized on a distinctive look.

The all-woman cast of *The Club* created an additional stage dynamic for director Tommy Tune.

Opposite:
The fabulous "Famous Feet" that Tommy Tune staged for *A Day in Hollywood/A Night in the Ukraine* belonged to Niki Harris and Albert Stevenson. Dancing on a platform suspended high above the stage, the two dancers impersonated Ruby Keeler and Dick Powell, an anonymous vaudeville act dancing to "Beyond the Blue Horizon," and Ginger Rogers and Fred Astaire. The ongoing number also presented the celebrated mice Mickey and Minnie, Tom Mix, Sonja Henie, Judy Garland, and Dracula.

make movement, musical staging, and dance all of a piece in a way that a team can only approximate. Moreover Prince, in staging *Evita* and *The Phantom of the Opera*, moved away from dance toward Andrew Lloyd Webber's operatic approach. "In shows like those," Tune says, "it's the scenery that's choreographed, the sets that keep moving. I loved *Phantom*, but I would personally rather have people moving." Tune, then, was virtually alone in continuing the development of the concept musical as an extension of choreographed direction. In a sense, this made for a good second phase, for as Jerome Robbins had bequeathed his artistic mantle to Fosse and Prince, and then Prince to Michael Bennett, so Tune was Bennett's protégé. Now this gentle giant loomed above Broadway as a kind of savior, not merely dreaming up musicals of fancy, but stretching traditional musical comedy limits toward a modern kind of musical theater that, while conceptual and balletic, was still *Broadway*. And where did he get these fanciful ideas?

Why, like Irving Berlin, he just got them out of thin air.

The theater of Tommy Tune is a life-affirming one, enthusiastically seeking after good feelings; it is a joyous and energetic theater that is ultimately justified by effect, with little concern for intellectual substance. Tune seeks to mesmerize his audience with fantastical pictures, and thus to entrance it. Magic is his intention, and a modestly defined artistry; his is the art of show business.

As the only important musicals director to be equally successful at staging drama, Tuned showed a versatility that was hardly to be anticipated from someone as inexperienced as he. Tune had been a chorus boy, a gangling tap dancer whose fey manner was incongruous with his six feet six inches. He had danced with the one-time model Twiggy in the movie version of *The Boy Friend*. He had appeared on Broadway in the 1973 *Seesaw*, winning a Tony Award as the best featured actor in a musical. His friend and mentor Michael Bennett had given him that job, asking him to choreograph his own numbers.

This could hardly have prepared him for a directing debut as astonishing as *The Club* in 1976. Eve Merriam's play was set in an elegant, private, turn-of-the-century men's club. There was music in it to be sure, but period songs did not make *The Club* a musical. By styling every inch of it, however, and choreographing every step of it, by making pictures of its every moment and coordinating the lighting, the set design, and the costumes with the patterns of floor movement, and even using such props as white gloves and ribbons for visual effect, Tune created two hours of dazzling stage imagery. In the end, this off-Broadway production was neither a play nor a musical but an exercise in style.

The decision to cast it with actresses cross-dressed in men's formal suits began a Tune pattern of unsettling audiences by capitalizing on startled expectations, whether in the form of costumes and props or confused gender. *The Club*, then, despite having no musical numbers as such, was ultimately more musical in feeling than many of the standard musical comedies that were on Broadway at the time.

And so Tommy Tune arrived as if some magician had conjured him up and he was a human genie, the kind Broadway desperately needed, one who could make the best kind of magic, for wonder of wonders, what emerged from his magic lantern were *hits*.

The illusion that Tommy
Tune devised for the celebrated "Angelettes March"
— real dancers and dolls —
in *The Best Little Whorehouse in Texas* was so
jealously guarded by the
show's producers that they
forbade any printed
pictures of it for the run
of the show.

"I didn't like the way dancers looked, showing up for auditions," Tommy Tune said about *The Best Little Whorehouse in Texas*, "so I just got all these old football boys and taught them how to do it."

101

A pensive star (Raul Julia) and his director (Tommy Tune) work out a moment for *Nine* in rehearsal.

From *The Club* in 1976 to *Grand Hotel* in 1990, Tune made six hits in seven tries, including four musicals, two plays with strong musical elements, and the acclaimed off-Broadway drama *Cloud Nine*, which seemed musical without the whisper of a song or the hint of a dance. Yet for all this productivity, he spent 1983 to 1987 not directing at all but starring in *My One and Only*, first on Broadway, then on national tour, and even in Japan. Between these travels he performed as a tap dancer in night clubs, on cruise ships, even in Catskill Mountains resort hotels, for he was in love with performing and that is one key to his work. The basic fact of theater is enough for Tommy Tune, and the giving of a show is its own justification. To *show*, in fact, is his stage purpose.

Thomas James Tune (his real name) is a Wichita Falls Texan, and his first Broadway chance came from fellow Texans, the authors of the 1978 musical *The Best Little Whorehouse in Texas*. Engaged as its choreographer and co-director, he devised a number that alone was virtually responsible for the show's success. Called "The Angelettes March," it was a line of cheerleaders with every other woman in the dance line actually a life-sized doll being supported by real dancers on either side. Like the cross-dressed "men" in *The Club*, these dolls were facetious illusions, not really meant to deceive but to amuse, the trick transparent. Tune realized how much audiences love to be a part of the theater game. His devices allowed them to respond as children without having their maturity insulted.

The Angelettes routine was the talk of the two-year run of *The Best Little Whorehouse in Texas*, and the success led to an assignment directing a pair of one-act musicals, *A Day in Hollywood/A Night in the Ukraine*, written by Richard Vosburgh and Frank Lazarus. The second half was a send-up of Marx Brothers movies, and for the quirky little revue that opened the show, Tune concocted a startling number that, like the cross-dressed women of *The Club* and the Angelettes in *The Best Little Whorehouse in Texas*, became the image by which the entire production would be known. This was "Famous Feet," showing such dancers as Fred Astaire and Ginger Rogers, Judy Garland, Mickey Mouse, Charlie Chaplin, Ruby Keeler, and Dick Powell, but only from the knees down. The impersonators performed high above the stage on a platform suspended from the top of the proscenium arch so that only their legs could be seen. It was an ingenious notion, and ingenuity was the Tune speciality.

His first outright Broadway musical was *Nine* in 1982. *Hollywood/Ukraine* had been a hybrid, two plays with songs rather than a full-scale musical. Because Broadway was such a desolate place in the early eighties, the show was nominated anyway for a Tony as the best musical of the year. It lost to *Evita*, but *Nine* was not only named the best musical of 1982, Tune took the prize for best director over his friend and mentor Michael Bennett (for *Dreamgirls*).

Nine with music and lyrics by Maury Yeston and a book by Arthur Kopit, is based on the Federico Fellini film *8½*. The movie was a masterpiece of hallucination, and fantastical visions were the Fellini speciality. It depicts the memories of a famed movie director, plainly Fellini himself, as he reflects on a career crisis, on his conflicting attitudes toward the Roman Catholic church, and on his lifelong obsession with women and the variety of them in his life.

Although the musical deals with the same material and likewise might be occurring in the main character's mind, Tune seemed less interested in this man than

Audiences gasped at Anita Morris's voluptuousness in *Nine*.

Raul Julia and Cameron Johann, playing his character's boyhood self, raise their batons.

in the imagery. If he identified with Fellini, it was in the realm of realized dreams and surreal presentations.

The essential visions in *Nine* are, first, a setting of blinding white tile against which there are black costumes and, second, a company of all women with but a single male. The location is the bathhouse of a Venetian spa where the director Guido Contini (Raul Julia) has come to recharge his psychic batteries so as to cope with a creative block. In this process, his life passes before him.

Tune engaged a company of twenty-one beautiful actresses to play the women in this limbo of memory, including Liliane Montevecchi as a movie producer, Karen Akers as Contini's wife, and the gorgeous likes of Anita Morris and Taina Elg as various lovers and mistresses. Uninterested in choreography as such, he hired another choreographer (Thommie Walsh) to work out the staging for the dances for *Nine*. In the end, only one was ever devised, and it was cut. Tune was much more interested in imagery than in movement at this time, and the result would be a static show.

Nine starts with Contini at center stage seated in a Zenlike position as the women of his life surround him and, like a symphony conductor, he rises to lead them in a wordless opening number that initiates a sequence of almost uninterrupted music, with the dialogue rhythmically chanted against a flowing orchestral underscore.

Tune is intensely aware of the importance of bravura beginnings, but once past this, *Nine* is haunted by an old-fashioned hobgoblin, the book. For any musical is dependent on that, whether it is simple entertainment or a show with high artistic aspirations. A structure simply must hold all the musical elements together, and in the case of *Nine*, it is even more important because there are so few musical numbers to distract the audience. What was it about? Where was its story? The questions are nagging, and, in fact, it is a show about imagery, and that isn't enough.

What story there is in *Nine* deals with the movie director's inability to make up his mind about what movie to do next. Should it be a western? A Bible epic? A documentary? It was not a crisis to grip an ordinary audience's attention for two hours. The critics were more easily absorbed. *Nine* was a prestigious success but not a popular one. There was a dazzling imagination at work, that was plain, and it made the show seem better than it really was, but this artistic aura did not satisfy an audience in search of a good show. Nevertheless *Nine* established Tommy Tune on Broadway.

The next year (1983), an avant-garde opera director named Peter Sellars (not to be confused with the late comedian) suggested that Tune return to performing as the star of *My One and Only*. The idea was to use the songs from *Funny Face*, the 1927 Gershwin vehicle for Fred and Adele Astaire, with a completely new libretto by Timothy S. Mayer and a great deal of tap dancing created and danced by Tune. Not much convincing was necessary. His directing career was thriving but he remained stagestruck and knew that he wouldn't always be young enough to sing and dance in musicals. "I adore that life," he said, "getting in a hit Broadway musical."

The few dances in *Nine* were staged by Thommie Walsh.

He convinced Sellars to hire Twiggy — a pal since *The Boy Friend* movie — as his co-star. But Broadway musicals are treacherous waters for new swimmers, and whatever were Peter Sellars's credentials as an opera director, he had almost no

experience in commercial theater. His version of the featherbrained Gershwin musical comedy was a dark and dour, neo-Brechtian work of Expressionistic theater about world economics and the Depression. Disaster couldn't wait for tryouts. It showed up during rehearsal. That was when the emergency troops arrived.

Peter Stone is one of Broadway's few professional book writers and in the 1980s emerged as its most reliable one. He is also one of Broadway's most successful show doctors. On these occasions he prefers to be called a "technician," but whatever the job description, the purpose is fixing an ailing musical. Ironically, Stone was also the president of the Dramatists Guild and in that capacity was a spokesman, advisor, and defender for the very librettist he was replacing on *My One and Only*. He advised Mayer of his rights as an author, rights that included protection against any unauthorized alteration of his work, including Peter Stone's. If Mayer chose, he could have closed *My One and Only* then and there, and he was reminded of that by Stone himself, but few make this choice, preferring to swallow pride and accept credit along with the "doctor" (technician) and the royalties. That was what Mayer preferred and work proceeded as other fixers arrived, led by director Mike Nichols.

Nichols is a curiosity in the musical theater. Ever since he stumbled while staging *The Apple Tree* in 1966, he has shied away from musicals to concentrate on being one of the best directors of comedies in Broadway history. As a co-producer of *Annie*, he provided so much sound advice that many credited him with shaping that

It was the original director, Peter Sellars, who came up with the notion of an all-black male ensemble dancing with an all-white female ensemble in *My One and Only*.

Tommy Tune suggested Twiggy as his co-star in *My One and Only*. They'd been friends since making the movie *The Boy Friend* together.

long-germinating, unsteady project into the great hit it finally became, but Nichols refused credit for it and continued to plead clumsiness with musicals. He was making that protest as he arrived on the scene of *My One and Only*.

But he moved quickly and with directness, stripping away the Brechtian devices and the social commentary. Sellars had sought a contrast between German Expressionism and Tune's bubbly tap dancing as set to the lilting Gershwin score. Nichols went after a consistently goofy atmosphere. Stone, meantime, reduced the story to a bold transatlantic flight and a sunny romance, retaining only the main characters from the script, Captain Billy Buck Chandler and the swimming star Edith Herbert. They were sketched out in bold cartoon strokes, while the minor role of Mr. Magix, played by the legendary tap dancer Charles "Honi" Coles, was expanded and exploited, becoming a mythic figure in a musical that no longer was about Expressionism. It was now about tap dancing.

One of the most original of Sellars' ideas was kept, the daring notion (in racially sensitive times) of casting the dancers with only black men and white women. The purpose was not only visual contrast but the sexual tension that would be subliminally created. Sellars realized that most audiences are middle-class people who feel uncomfortable with interracial romance. Aside from that, the main hold-over from the Sellars version of *My One and Only* was the music, such Gershwin classics as "'S Wonderful," "He Loves and She Loves," and of course the title song. Ira Gershwin was convinced to allow the addition of songs from other shows, and the musical numbers began to increase. Tune, of course, had to choreograph the new material, including "Strike Up the Band" and "Nice Work If You Can Get It."

Using old songs created its own problems. One of the great attractions of a new show is the new songs that come to identify it. Tune urged his dance pianist, Wally Harper, to make the music fresh with unusual arrangements, and an arrangement indeed can do that — make new with a novel vamp (the opening figures) or a unique development and performance notion.

The difference between an arrangement and an orchestration is sometimes blurred because the terms are used interchangeably in movie and record production, where the same person usually arranges and orchestrates. But in the theater, an arrangement is worked out during rehearsal, between the choreographer and the dance pianist, to be orchestrated later. The arrangement determines precisely how the song is to be routined — it is the organizing and structuring of the number that decides what key it is to be sung in, what harmonies are to be used, what rhythms, how many voices, and what dance breaks will occur. The orchestration is the setting of this music to instrumentation.

Michael Gibson wrote the wonderful orchestrations for *My One and Only*, but Wally Harper wrote the arrangements that began to make these familiar Gershwin songs seem fresh and theatrical and right for this show, even though they had not been written for it. Audiences knew the songs but they didn't know them to sound like this, and *My One and Only* could thus sound in period but new.

With the show now in condition to open out of town, Nichols left and Michael Bennett came to apply a final polish. Instead, however, *My One and Only* abruptly lurched into chaos. The company became confused and shaky. Many believed that Bennett was deliberately betraying his friend Tommy Tune out of a continuing pique over having lost the Tony Award for his *Dreamgirls* to Tune's *Nine*. At week's end Bennett was dismissed, leaving Tune as not only the star and the choreographer, but as the director as well.

He continued staging the added Gershwin songs, and the show's spirits were so giddy that any song *could* be added, with little concern for the lyrics' relevance, for no relevance was necessary when the point of view could be summed up as

> Bad news go 'way
> Call 'round some day
> In March or May,
> I'm dancing and I can't be bothered now.

By the time *My One and Only* arrived on Broadway (May 1, 1983), it was another Tommy Tune original. Despite the various contributors and all the emergencies, this musical had visual style and a sunniness that was radiantly contagious. Audiences adored it, and *My One and Only* ran more than two years on Broadway and then across the country and on to Tokyo. Tommy Tune had a box office touch but, more important, there was a promise of real artistry to come.

It would come with *Grand Hotel*.

The fleeting and stylish image of Fred Astaire has haunted all male dancers and Tune understandably jumped at the chance to dance like the master.

Director Tommy Tune's
introduction of the
company brings the central
characters downstage.

6
THE MAKING OF A MUSICAL: GRAND HOTEL

One middle-of-the-night in 1983, Tommy Tune awoke to find the Greta Garbo–John Barrymore classic *Grand Hotel* playing on the television screen. Next morning he called Maury Yeston, who had written the songs for his then-current hit, *Nine,* to suggest musicalizing the film. The composer declined, but through the years Tune thought about the idea and read the 1927 Vicki Baum novel *Menschen im Hotel,* on which the stage play and movie had been based.

He was not alone in imagining *Grand Hotel* as a musical. In fact, a libretto and score already existed, the script by Luther Davis and the songs by Robert Wright and George Forrest, who had previously collaborated on the hit musical *Kismet.* But *Kismet* was a 1953 show and Wright and Forrest's other success was even older, *Song of Norway* in 1944.

Still, when their *Grand Hotel* musical was submitted to Martin Richards and Sam Crothers, the producers were excited about its possibilities, and, hearing about Tune's longstanding interest in the idea, they got in touch with him.

He not only found the script old-fashioned, but worse, he learned that *it had already been produced* — thirty years earlier in Los Angeles, where it had flopped under the title *At the Grand.*

The authors insisted that it had since been rewritten, but the only changes were a return from Rome to the novel's original Berlin setting and a restoring of the leading lady as a ballet dancer (she had been made into an opera diva). Yet Tune was not discouraged. It seemed eerily possible to him that *Grand Hotel* might be the musical that belonged in a setting he had been recurringly dreaming about.

Santo Loquasto created this elegant dress and cape for the ballerina, Elizaveta.

At top:
Tune begins to work with the movable revolving door.

Above:
Rehearsal pianists work out the musical fabric that links a musical's songs and creates continuity. Ultimately, the music in *Grand Hotel* would be nearly continuous. Director Tune had said, "I wanted to focus the audience but at the same time to have the rest of the show in action all the time."

I would be in this shiny-floored ballroom with a parquet floor and a chandelier and these gilded chairs with red velvet cushions lined up all around the room, and I would be standing there thinking, "This would be a good place to make a show." And that was the end of the dream.

If that was to be, however, the play would have to be completely remade, for he did not want anything like this linear script that moved from one scene to the next hauling realistic scenery in its lumbering wake. He told Luther Davis, the librettist, "I just don't want to move in a whole set of the bedroom and then have to bring in the whole spiral staircase into the lobby and then bring in the bandstand. We'll be there all night. Besides," he added, referring to the current Broadway rage for extravaganzas, "I don't want to do another designer musical. Let's do a workshop so you can see what I mean."

Tune's mentor, Michael Bennett, had popularized the "workshopping" of musicals with *A Chorus Line*. It meant the making of a show in a practice-room situation, through trial and error, instead of staging a scripted work. This evolved from the realization that no musicals were finished until they were performed. Workshops were expensive, with actors on a payroll, but producers learned to consider that a worthwhile expenditure. A workshop production could better demonstrate a musical's viability than a script could, and money was more easily raised by inviting potential investors to see a show with actors, costumes, and lighting than through backers' auditions with the authors singing around a piano in a living room. Moreover, a project could be cancelled should the workshop fail, and while the expense (around $200,000 in 1989) was as great as a whole show used to be, it was still less than the four or five million dollars that would be lost on a Broadway flop.

On January 27, 1989, after hiring Wally Harper to be the all-important musical supervisor and rehearsal pianist who would transform the songs into musical fabric, and with Jack Lee as vocal director, Tune began to audition actors. He didn't bother with dance auditions because he didn't yet know how much dancing there was going to be. His first concern was the book, for he knew how many shows with great musical numbers had failed because of weak scripts.

The libretto that he envisioned was an impressionistic one. He wanted to use Luther Davis's words "but not in the order they were written." He wanted that script "scrambled," its dialogue fractured so that "scenes begin before others end," and he needed actors who could contribute to this creative process. According to one of them, "Tommy was not only intuitive about us, but probably psychic"—for the company would ultimately understand where the show in their director's mind was heading and how to help it get there.

Tune found a work place, the ballroom of the seedy Hotel Diplomat off Times Square. He didn't want to use a Broadway rehearsal studio "because I don't like to rehearse in a place with mirrors. That's a place for making dances, not shows." Uncannily, the Diplomat's ballroom was almost a replica of the ballroom in his recurring dream, with a parquet floor, four columns in its middle, a chandelier, and

even gilded chairs along the periphery. "It was tacky," he conceded, especially after having been converted into a discotheque, "but it still had vestiges of grandeur, and the columns made it look like a three-ring circus. Things could go on outside the columns, and inside is the center ring."

The first day of work, March 16, 1989, he told the assembled actors, dance pianist, vocal director, and authors, "We're going to do a workshop for six weeks and then we're going to see whether or not we have a show." He was aware that hard work, even good work, brought no guarantee of produceable work. His friend Michael Bennett had workshopped *Scandals* for almost two years and then, when it became clear that it wasn't working, scrapped it.

As the producers of *Grand Hotel* (its workshop at least) left the ballroom to the showmakers that winter afternoon, Tune sat down, front-to-back on one of the gilt chairs and extended his endless, cowboy-booted legs. He was not passing out the script. ("It was too old-fashioned, too creaky.") He told the company, "In television, audiences have learned to watch in short takes. I want a collage. Let's make this like pointillism." He was an amateur painter and liked to use art for his analogies.

The opening of a musical, and most will agree with Tune, "is the hardest thing in the world," whisking the audience in from the street and depositing it in a wonderland where singing and dancing are part of normal life. It is a critical juncture, setting the tone of a show and introducing its world, its characters, catching the audience's fancy, or losing its interest irretrievably. Tune wanted nothing of traditional opening numbers. "I didn't want a lot of people dancing across the stage." He had something more ambitious in mind, a progression from Sondheim and Prince's *Follies* and Bennett's *A Chorus Line*, and from his own *Nine;* he envisioned

Above:
Another costume sketch by Santo Loquasto.

Above, left:
Grand Hotel was developed in workshops held in the ballroom of the Hotel Diplomat in New York City. The ballroom's chairs along the sides inspired the show's "Berliner Ensemble," and later these same chairs would become an inanimate dance company, to be arranged and rearranged in kaleidoscopic floor patterns.

111

The Baron lights up Flaemmchen.

a dreamlike concept musical presenting not the substance but the spirit of a great hotel where "there's always something happening," like the lobby of the elegant hotel in Monte Carlo, where he had just finished a personal appearance.

He set to work on an opening sequence that would introduce the six central characters who have crises in common with each other — and in contrast to the luxurious setting of the Berlin hotel. These characters are the young and handsome Baron Felix Von Gaigern, who must steal to hold off his dangerous creditors; the ballerina Elizaveta Grushinskaya, fearing age and the end of her dancing career, despite the sympathy of her adoring secretary Raffaela; the mortally ill bookkeeper Otto Kringelein, who is looking for a final taste of life; the typist Frieda Flaemm, who, in her poverty, fantasizes about going to Hollywood and becoming a movie star; and the businessman Preysing, whose stockholders are on the verge of dismissing him as General Director.

They are all shareholders in desperation, and Tune meant to project that at the outset, in a theatrically orchestrated sequence that would not only introduce them as characters but, as he put it, "define the style of the show."

He gave each a few lines to play with and seated them at "telephones" in the center of the ballroom. The ballerina's companion Raffaela is trying to pawn her needy mistress's jewels; the bookkeeper Kringelein is calling the hospital to confess that he has fled; the typist Frieda is telling a boyfriend that she is pregnant; Preysing is calling his wife in a panic about his business situation; and the Baron is trying to pacify his violent creditors.

At the piano, Wally Harper played a lightly rhythmic version of one of the Wright and Forrest songs. The team's previous shows had drawn themes from Borodin and Grieg, but this was original music, quite attractive and, in Harper's ingeniously improvised arrangements, it sounded fresh and ingratiating. He extrapolated from the melodies, developing variations. ("Wally would take this music," Tune said, "and take it places they never thought of.")

Tune suggested that the actors feel free to break up and interweave their lines, to echo each other. He urged them to be aware of a time pressure on these characters. "Quickly" was an important word, and a key phrase was "time is running out." So they took to the telephones in the lobby of the Grand Hotel on the bare floor of the seedy ballroom and began to make a show.

> RAFFAELA
> Quickly.
> KRINGELEIN
> I was in ward three last night.
> RAFFAELA
> Quickly.
> FLAEMM
> I need money.
> KRINGELEIN
> Quickly. I haven't time.
> FLAEMM
> I'm late. By only a few weeks but I'm usually like a Swiss clock.

PREYSING

Yes. It's Daddy. All the way from Berlin. Let me speak to Mommy.

BARON

I have to speak to you about money.

Harper, playing the piano underneath these snatches of telephone conversation, picked up his tempo.

RAFFAELA

Quickly.

KRINGELEIN

Is waiting.

PREYSING

No radiogram! Time is running out.

KRINGELEIN

And I have so little time. Dr. Kaufman? I'm not coming back to the hospital. I'm at—

"Grand Hotel!" the watching actors shouted, as Tune had planned, and Harper erupted into full chords at the piano. The readings, too, grew more intense and became musical in their counterpoint.

The Baron (David Carroll) dances with Flaemmchen (Jane Krakowski). Nearly perpetual choreography makes *Grand Hotel* a unique kind of theater ballet. Many of the dancers have no partners in this stylized fox trot, but the audience accepts the choreography as part of the show's underlying rhythm, like musical underscoring.

113

Mortally ill, Kringelein arrives at the *Grand Hotel*, hoping for one taste, at last, of luxury.

BARON

I need a little more time. I understand. Time *is* running out.

FLAEMM

No, women don't catch cold there. All we catch down there is pregnant.

RAFFAELA

Madam does not go out in daylight. You must come to Grand Hotel. Today. Time is running out.

PREYSING

No! Not for the Preysing family is there such a thing as "bankruptcy."

FLAEMM

Just send the money! It cannot wait. Time is running out.

And at the piano Harper played still more dramatically.

KRINGELEIN

I just cashed in my savings, Doctor. Time is running out.

Tune urged his actors to be unafraid of overlapping each other yet to make sure they could be understood. "Do it like radio," he said. "Radio show it," by which he meant that they should create pictures through words, pictures so vivid that a radio audience could grasp them, so clear that "even a baby could understand it. I'm listening like a baby," he told them, "I'm trying to make sense of something I've never heard before." He knew that for every audience, each performance was the first performance.

"Radio show it" would become a familiar suggestion. "We would radio show a sequence and, soon as it sounded right, I would stage it. It was a synthesis," Tune said.

From eleven in the morning until six o'clock each evening, the work continued, and after that first week he felt that he had created ten minutes of material. Only then did he invite the producers into the Hotel Diplomat's ballroom. At a quarter-past six on the Friday of the first week, for the first time, the ten-minute *Grand Hotel* was performed and the show had begun.

Ten minutes of a Broadway musical can take an eternity to create and seem even longer when going wrong. The only way ten minutes can play as they should — in an instant — is for every moment to be controlled, making for a density of materials, no time wasted. Instead of being intimidated by this requirement, Tune was inspired. "*Grand Hotel* is going to be a ballet," he told librettist Luther Davis, not meaning a literal ballet, because he still didn't know how much dance there would be, but that the dance was never to stop. Michael Bennett had once talked to him about doing shows that were wall-to-wall with musical numbers, never pausing for applause — so visually communicative that words were unnecessary. Tune needed words to tell this story, he said to the (grateful) librettist, but he was not going to stop for applause, and he wanted snatches of dialogue from different scenes and different characters in different areas of the hotel, creating the impressionistic canvas he envisioned. Luther Davis's script was hardly written that way. Tune was going to plunder every draft besides the original Vicki Baum novel and even her memoirs to find the verbal daubs for the pointillism he imagined, and in this painstaking way, a performance structure would be built, a music-dance-drama with a continuous rhythm, a musical aura, and a painterly expanse.

In the second week of the workshop, pianist Wally Harper began to under-score some of the dialogue with connective music while vocal director Jack Lee blended couplets from some of the songs into the dialogue. Tune let the actors improvise movement and incorporated some of that into his developing panorama — a girl who walks drunkenly across the hotel lobby; the manager shooing away the shabby, fragile Kringelein. In the meanwhile, Harper continued to extrapolate musical fabric from the basic Wright and Forrest songs.

In that second week, Tune introduced "circling." This was a ritual conducted every day before the start of work. The company would form a circle to hold hands and "think healing thoughts." Tommy Tune was not a bliss ninny skipping light-heartedly toward cosmic consciousness, although he did believe in high spirits. Not everyone in the company, however, shared a taste for holding hands and thinking healing thoughts. Tune shrugged his shoulders and suggested that such cynics "play in the baseball league," meaning the spring Broadway League softball games in Central Park (which were implicitly for the macho — the athletes). In fact, he needed healing thoughts himself as his mother was dying at home in Houston and he knew he would be flying there at the end of every week.

He built on the first ten minutes. "Paint it," he would say about the pan-demonium in the hotel lobby. "Let that line come down and this one bubble up." Taking a cue from the opening of the movie, *Grand Hotel*, he introduced the sounds of telephones and desk bells ringing, of switchboard operators and bellhops paging guests and managers giving orders. He began calling the ensemble of chorus people "the Berliner Ensemble" after the famous theater company of Bertolt Brecht. "Think of our show," he said, "as if we are in 1928 with Brecht and the Berliner Ensemble."

The ballerina Elizaveta (Liliane Montevecchi) is flattered by her adoring manager and theater owner.

"But Tommy," one of the chorus people said, "we aren't the Berliner Ensemble. We're the *Irving* Berliner Ensemble."

Humor is the eternal relief and not long after that laughter, some of the gypsies (chorus dancers) began calling the show *Nein*.

There were dancers in the company even though there had been no dance auditions because Tune knew that there was eventually going to be some dancing. The first real use of it, the first outright musical number, was "Maybe My Baby Loves Me," performed by a couple of bartenders (both named "Jimmy") in 1920s jazz style. In keeping with the aim of avoiding realistic scenery and stretching the audience's imagination, he gave the two Jimmies a length of ballet barre to represent a counter. He had used a similar pole as a visual device in *Nine*. Now the barre would come to play a more versatile role, ultimately serving as this counter, or a row of wash basins in the hotel lounge, or a purely visual device for dance numbers.

The singing and dancing in "Maybe My Baby Loves Me" is done as Frieda Flaemm looks on, although by then she has changed her name to "Flaemmchen" in hope of a Hollywood career. The reality of her sad life ("in Friedrichstrasse where if something gets broken it stays broken") is that she is poor and pregnant, and although she is smitten with the handsome young Baron, he has fallen in love with Elizaveta, the ballet dancer. Flaemmchen decides to settle for being kept by the businessman Preysing and agrees to go with him to Boston which, he assures her, is "only a train ride away" from Hollywood.

Tune kept adding tiles to his mosaic, gluing in story details with movement and music. He permitted a dramatic dawdle only for the central romance between the Baron (David Carroll) and the ballerina (Liliane Montevecchi). And as the workshop's second week ended, he made it plain that he was serious about short-circuiting any applause. That was a tough decision because everyone in the theater

116

thrives on audience approval, but in *Dreamgirls*, Michael Bennett had even stopped the audience from applauding the show's dramatic peak (the song, "And I Am Telling You I'm Not Going") by moving directly into another musical number. Bennett was convinced that applause breaks a musical's momentum, and Tune listened when Michael Bennett taught.

In Houston, he "told" the show to his failing mother, describing every dramatic device and every song. He told her about the ballerina discovering the cat burglar Baron in her room and falling in love with him, in that process recovering her desire to dance. He told about Preysing leering after Flaemmchen, lying to save his collapsing business, catching the Baron stealing his wallet and shooting him. When Tune's mother asked about choreography, he said he was going to use period dances such as the fox trot and the tango. "My mother was a flapper," he later said. "She knew all those dances better than anyone." He also mulled over the idea of using the "surround"—the chairs along the walls of the ballroom—and when he returned to New York, he told the company that the Berliner Ensemble would be scattered along those chairs where they would watch the action and respond in what he called their "peripheral lives."

"Are we part of it?" one of them asked.

"Can the characters see us?"

"Are we characters or are we ourselves?"

"You tell me," he impishly said. "Tell me what my idea is."

And so they spread themselves on the chairs along the ballroom walls miming, chatting, gesturing toward the characters in the scenes, embracing or just watching as the frail Kringelein strikes up a friendship with the Baron, who suggests that he try a fox trot with Flaemmchen. As David Carroll, playing the Baron, suavely put a cigarette in his mouth, his lighter failed. One of the actors on the periphery jumped up and gave him a light.

"Keep that!" Tune cried with a snap of his fingers.

Kringelein hardly seems strong enough to get through the dance and protests that he does not know how to do the fox trot, but Flaemmchen sings

Who wouldn't dance with you
You sweep a lady off her feet, mister!

Behind them, Tune was gathering a dozen dancers and setting them on the Grand Hotel dance floor, moving the group as a stylized ensemble. He let this precision fox trot continue behind Flaemmchen and Kringelein and the Baron in their scene, not as a musical number but as a visual counterpoint, a choreographic underscoring. As the scene evolved, he even asked Wally Harper to stop playing the piano. Moving those dancers in cross-passing lines, he let their shuffling feet become the bed of sound on which the scene played. The businessman Preysing is now demanding that Flaemmchen type the speech he is preparing for his stockholders, and Kringelein, suddenly showing an unaccustomed courage, angrily responds that she will finish her dance with him first.

The manager of the *Grand Hotel* pays off a blackmailer.

Another week into the workshop and Tune added the thirty-two gilt chairs with the red velvet seats to the deepening show picture. He would find somewhere else for the periphery characters to sit. He knew why these chairs had been in his dream. There had been symmetrical chairs in *Nine*. Now he decided to "pick up where I had left off" and set the chairs "in the exact configuration of *Nine*. You start with your last painting and make up your next painting." These chairs would become an inanimate dance company, endlessly rearranged throughout *Grand Hotel*, kaleidoscopic Busby Berkeley chairs.

Meantime, he was concerned about Liliane Montevecchi's new song, which he had asked for and not yet received. Still waiting for it, he began work with a quartet of scullery workers who would represent the hotel's have-nots. One of these workers was played by Henry Grossman, an acclaimed photographer who in his heart wanted to be a singer in a Broadway musical. *Grand Hotel* was his first chance and he took it, as well as some of the photographs on these pages.

As the workshop progressed through the fifth week, Tune warned the troupe that "the suits" would soon be coming. The suits were the money people, potential investors. The six o'clock audiences had already begun to grow. Downy-cheeked executives from Paramount Pictures were coming regularly, "and we began seeing 'people,'" one of the actors remembered, meaning recognizable show folk like José Ferrer and Mike Nichols. The room was actually getting crowded, an audience watching what was now more than forty minutes of a musical. A decision about its fate would soon be at hand.

Tune didn't seem nervous the day that everything he'd made, fifty minutes of *Grand Hotel*, was to be shown to the suits and the producers and whomever else the producers had invited. As usual, the company thought its healing thoughts before work, and then Tune said, "Okay guys, we've got to clean up our mess today. I'm deliberately closing my ears to what you're saying so that when I see confusing things, I know what to clean up." And after he watched a run-through he sat them down and gave them notes. Then he said, "Okay, now I'm going to deliberately close my *eyes* to what you're *doing* so that when I don't understand what you're *saying* I'll know what to clean up." And they did the fifty-minute show again, and again he gave them notes.

At six o'clock the audience began to arrive, more than a hundred people. It was time for the workshop to conclude and for the real *Grand Hotel* to start.

"Well, we're going to Boston," Tune told the company, and everyone cheered except Flaemmchen, Fay Grant, because she was as pregnant as her character. She was replaced by the 22-year-old Jane Krakowski. The other leading actors were retained—Liliane Montevecchi as the ballerina, Karen Akers as her secretary, Raffaela, David Carroll as the Baron, Michael Jeter as Kringelein, and Timothy Jerome as Preysing, the businessman. Tune had hoped that everyone in the company would be offered a "principal" contract and be treated equally. "You are all figures in a painting," he had told them, "and in a painting, all figures are important." But Actors Equity, the union, was not interested in paintings and ruled that there were obvious principal roles and obvious ensemble assignments. Eventually, everyone would at least be treated as equals in the program and listed in alphabetical order.

In Boston for the tryout, Tune continued making the show and "scrambling" the original script of Luther Davis. He had asked the composers, Wright and Forrest, for a new song that Preysing could sing about lying to his stockholders, and they wrote "Take the Crooked Path," a quirky and striking fable; but with the world premiere fast approaching, they had not yet done anything about the song for Montevecchi. When Tune asked for that yet again, one of them replied, "Johnny Mercer once advised us, 'A couplet a day, a couplet a day.'"

"Listen guys," Tune said patiently, "Johnny Mercer and his couplets a day weren't in Boston with a musical that was going to bomb. We need a whole bunch of songs, fellas. Let's get to work."

Most urgently needed was a song and dance in which the Baron and the mortally ill Kringelein would celebrate their friendship. Tune had already stepped up the dancing ("The show was taking on its own life by then") and had made a tap dance for Kringelein — "We called it 'the German Tap.' It was charming and it was fun and everybody liked it and it was just *wrong*."

The ballerina wants to accept the word of the Baron that he has come to her room not as a thief but as a lover.

Remembering his commitment to period social dances he thought, "Now what's the most celebratory dance of the period?

"The polka!"

But he planned to have Kringelein so carried away that after beginning the dance with the Baron he would spin off by himself, wildly and exuberantly. The polka, Tune realized, could not be danced alone. "And then I thought, my God! This is the era of the Charleston!"

And so Wright and Forrest wrote, "We'll Take a Glass Together," which the music supervisor Wally Harper developed into a rousing Charleston. He telefaxed the arrangement to the show's orchestrator, Peter Matz, in New York. This was a bit of computer-age technology in the gaslight world of Broadway. Even in the recent past, orchestrators would scribble through the nights in out-of-town hotel rooms, feverishly writing out the parts for all the musicians. Between travel expenses, per-diem pay and overtime, the cost of orchestrations had become a major burden on a musical's budget. With the phenomenon of fax machines, this laborious work (every musical part for every member of the pit band is hand-written) could at least be done in New York and during working hours without losing time.

The rest of the out-of-town experience was the same old craziness. Even in a fax world, show business remained as feverish and as lunatic as ever, and that was a relief.

Flying to Houston only days before the Boston opening, Tune tried out the Charleston on his dying mother. "I believe," he would later say, "that the whole number had something to do not only with Kringelein dying but with my mother too . . . and seeing her waste away." And without fail, every time that Kringelein spun away from the Baron to Charleston almost uncontrollably, the audience cheered for the indomitability of the human spirit, with not a few tears in the house.

The choreography was now seeking out and filling the show's every corner. There was dancing by the principals as part of the story, dancing by the ensemble downstage as part of the main event, or upstage as background; there was musical staging of the songs, in good cheer or dark and mocking. *Grand Hotel* was becoming through-danced, much as the Andrew Lloyd Webber shows were through-sung. It was beginning to throb.

Vicki Baum's message in the original novel had been that human beings are meaningless specks in the cosmic continuum while existence proceeds, oblivious to individual tragedy — "life goes on in the Grand Hotel." Tune gave that line to his narrator, the Colonel-Doctor, but, wisely, left it at that. He could not worry about the meaning of life. He had his hands full with a musical.

He added still more dancing: an adagio team, Yvonne Marceau and Pierre Dulaine, to dance a bolero as he saw them do it in a New York hotel. Dubbing them "The Countess and The Gigolo," he decided that they would "portray a memory of things gone." They would slither in and out like ghosts, flashing hints of their dance until at the end they fulfilled their promise and (she in black satin, his dark hair slicked down — Tune was shameless) they performed the complete "Love-Death Pas de Deux," a melodramatic bolero.

Wally Harper developed its music from a ballad sung earlier, transforming it into a thumping passion dance as Marceau and Dulaine coiled and slinked from one end of the stage to the other. Tune made the mysterious and silent pair stranger still, The Countess blind and The Gigolo supplying her with cocaine.

Hallucination had been in the air ever since Tune had described the show as being "like a dream." The first character on stage, even before the long opening sequence, is the Colonel-Doctor, the narrator, who injects himself with morphine while lights brighten and fall behind him. Some of the actors thought those lights indicated the start of a trance. Certainly there were other suggestions of drugged visions in the show's pictures, its fragmented reality, the surreal dancers, the height-ened imagery, the ghostly ballroom of Tony Walton's setting and Jules Fisher's dramatic lighting. Some in the company persisted in thinking of the whole show as a drug-induced hallucination that began with the doctor's needle. Tune himself had explained the needle as being there "because I wanted to alter the audience's state" — and what did that mean? "Altered state?" He steadfastly denied any connection between the show's dreamlike pictures and drug-induced hallucinations.

As the Boston premiere approached, his restless rearrangements of the thirty-two gilt chairs achieved a complex brilliance, their patterns myriad and precise. There was now a banquette wrapped around the sides and the back of the stage to seat the periphery actors. Otherwise, Tony Walton's setting was modeled on the ballroom of the Hotel Diplomat, with an upper level added for the orchestra to play in full view (the actors watched conductor Jack Lee on television screens suspended over the audience).

Just before the opening, Tune flew to Houston to see his mother for the last time. He told her *Grand Hotel*, the whole show, from beginning to end.

The first night in Boston was shocking. "Everything that had been wonderful in the workshop," Tune recalled, "was awful on the stage." The show he had thought so painterly, so metaphoric, so compassionate and rich and artistic only seemed hollow, shallow, and facile. While the unenthusiastic reviews were at least encourag-

Above, and opposite: The Baron and Kringelein (Michael Jeter) dance the heartwarming, show-stopping Charleston "We'll Take a Glass Together." Because the orchestra is on the upper deck, the cast takes its cues from the conductor by looking at television monitors suspended from the balcony.

ing rather than mean spirited (one critic even sent over a list of suggestions), Tune was influenced most by what the audience told him.

They told him that they wanted to applaud. "It wasn't fair to deny them that," he concluded, and so he began to create as many chances as he could. At a company meeting in the ladies' lounge, he announced that whenever possible there would be a "button" at the end of a musical number, which was the traditional cue for applause, and he would create a pause to give the audience time for that.

There are some directors who respond to crisis by pulling out their show-business tricks and discarding the original purpose in a frenzied effort at rescue and success. But Tommy Tune's response was to go deeper into the original vision, deeper than he had ever thought about. He decided to create a beginning before the already ambitious beginning—to expand further the opening sequence—and this was to be called "The Presentation of the Company." It would give the audience a chance to cheer at the very start.

He put in the calls for the New York show doctors, Maury Yeston, who had composed the music for *Nine*, and Peter Stone, who had been the "technician" (as he preferred calling it), who rewrote the libretto for Tune's *My One and Only*.

Stone set to work helping Davis define characters and tighten the dramatic exchanges in the overall collage. Tune had always said that he wanted the script cinematic, with quick cuts from one scene to the next. Stone was not only an experienced librettist but an Academy Award–winning screenwriter.

Work was intense as daily performances continued. Davis, Wright, and Forrest now were seldom to be seen. They told a visiting friend, "As soon as you see the opening, you'll know it's not our show." Yeston began writing the music for the Presentation—an achy, insinuating, mysteriously unforgettable theme song, "At the Grand Hotel." The music was lush and expansive, ringing with Old World luxury, and yet it had the minor key, the descending melody, and the melancholy chord changes that undercut the sense of this rich life with world weariness, and a certain doom.

"The Presentation of the Company," as Tune conceived it, "sets the scene and introduces the characters." One by one, they march to the audience. Flaemmchen, for instance, curtsies flirtatiously while the Baron bows romantically. Wally Harper's arrangement of the Yeston songs builds the number to a crowning, almost dizzying crest; then it subsides and leads into the ringing telephones and pinging counter bells of the original opening sequence, counterpointing countless cries of "Grand Hotel at your service" that, as Tune had said, "bubble up and down, painted in." It all came to a boil with the paging of guests, the cries of bellhops, the orders of the manager. As the Presentation reached its thrilling conclusion with the entire company lined up along the front of the stage and the orchestra roaring against a pounding clang, Tune had created an unprecedented stretch of music theater, every element orchestrated in a theater concerto.

So the stage was set by these curtain calls at the start, and with this engulfing stretch of theater, the audience was swept into the created world of the stage.

But could the multifaceted panorama be sustained? Would the audience be held within the vision?

Tune scanned his show for slow spots as it was performed. Whenever it would lag he would say, "Let's get some movement there" — and for a show whose dancing had been an unknown quantity at the start, it was becoming the most completely and densely choreographed musical in Broadway history, surpassing even *West Side Story*. It was becoming a show with endlessly changing images, its details revealing themselves evermore like a slowly revolving and evolving kaleidoscope. "The music never stops at the Grand Hotel," Vicki Baum had written, and as Tune had used the line in the show, now it was true.

He even dared violate such basic stage rules as never moving on the center of action. For instance during the big love scene between the ballerina and the Baron, he had frozen the actors on the periphery so as not to distract, but the audience seemed restless. So he suggested, "Let's have some passion on the surround," figuring that if attention wandered from the main love scene, there would be other love scenes to complete a romantic choreography. Maury Yeston, meantime, produced an ardent ballad, "Love Can't Happen," for the Baron to sing. David Carroll had the big voice to send it ringing through the theater.

Now running a tight two hours and ten minutes with no intermission, *Grand Hotel* was ready for Broadway — it hoped.

The days of glittering first nights had long since passed when this show brought them back with a fancy and glamorous crowd pushing past popping flash-bulbs on the night of its New York premiere, November 12, 1989. People had started going to Broadway opening nights in jeans and sweaters, but not on this occasion. This night at the Martin Beck Theatre on West 45th Street, there were men in dinner suits and women wearing jewels.

Their buzz and chatter subsided with the tapping of the conductor's baton high above the stage, whose skeletal structures were already exposed. Then a towering doorman strode downstage to grasp a freestanding revolving door and shove it all the way to the back so that the company might enter.

But the elaborately conceived "Presentation of the Company" did not, as planned, overwhelm this audience, nor did the long opening sequence that followed — not even with the scenic coup of three glittering chandeliers descending as they turned, down through the musicians' level to the main floor. In fact, there was no real ovation until Michael Jeter swung away from David Carroll to dance the Charleston by himself, and then the audience roared for the moment and the humanity of the sickly character's pyrotechnical dancing.

The critics were largely affirmative, and some recognized the musical theater milestone that *Grand Hotel* had struck, but generally Tune's production effects received higher grades than the story and songs.

It seemed as if the tremendous accomplishment might go unrecognized, especially after the show survived only fair attendance in hope of a business-boosting award in June; and then it lost the Tony for the year's best musical to *City of Angels* (although Tune won as Best Director). *Grand Hotel* was threatening to be a succès d'estime without even the esteem.

And then something wonderful happened. The segment that had been shown on national television during the Tony Awards generated business at the box office the next morning. Audiences grew rapturous. A line of customers became a fixture at the theater, and as they waited they compared notes on how many times they'd seen the show. The producers began to organize additional companies for productions in California, London, Tokyo, and, yes, Berlin. *Grand Hotel* was taking its rightful place among the great Broadway musicals, those that succeeded both artistically and commercially. It was becoming the stuff of legend, too, for more than any show in recent times, it had the thrill, the excitement, the chill and ache and unique electricity that had always been the exclusive character of Broadway musicals. Whatever changes were happening in this ever-dying, ever-surviving show business, *Grand Hotel* was a real Broadway musical, a musical as Broadway musicals had always been, perhaps extrapolated and evolved to a new size, dimension, and artistry. *Grand Hotel* was not quite the metaphor for life that Vicki Baum had novelized, but it was certainly a testament to show business, which perhaps was just as well, and provided a kind of greatness too.

And Tommy Tune, who seemed to believe in Broadway in a foolish and hopelessly demented way — who really believed that he had a responsibility to musical theater, being the last surviving choreographer-director — Tune had raised glitter to artistry, in the process making the show he was supposed to make in the ghostly, deserted ballroom of his dreams.

CHAPTER

7

CAMERON
MACKINTOSH

*In the end, people's passion to enjoy
shows, to produce and direct and write
musicals, is what matters. In the end, the
success of the people who've done musicals comes because to wake up in the
morning and* not *do musicals would kill
them. And it's got nothing to do, in
the end, with money.*
— Cameron Mackintosh

God knew not what he had wrought
when he wrought Broadway musicals. New York's theatergoers perhaps thought that
this was their special domain, but original-cast albums had created a race of the
young stagestruck, a race that was national and even transatlantic.

Like so many of those stagestruck, the young Cameron Mackintosh, growing
up in North London, could not bear the thought that Broadway musicals might
disappear before he might have a crack at them. And he very much feared that they
were going to disappear. Perhaps the Americans were too sure of their baby, or
perhaps those tending it were growing too old or too jaded to care. But in London,
where a young theater dreamer could only hear the latest Broadway shows on albums
that were unendurably slow in coming over, and where there was constant frustra-
tion by inadequate British productions that were years late, the lust for the real thing
remained passionate.

Mackintosh was barely out of his teens when he took to the theatrical road as a
sweeper, a prop boy, an assistant stage manager, and occasionally a chorus singer.
"Obsessed with American musicals," as he put it, he cut his producing teeth on
provincial repertory and worked his way up to producing his very own disaster, a
revival of *Anything Goes*, which taught him, "It isn't great songs that make a musical.
It's great books." It was a lesson that anyone doing musicals had to learn.

Consoled by the advice that if he could survive this two-week disaster he
could survive in the theater, he began producing new musicals. "For a Brit," he would
later say, "I was born at just the right time to bridge the end of the American musical
in its most flourishing period. I was able to see *The Music Man, Sweet Charity*, all those
really smart and top-drawer American musicals."

Ann McNeely and the
company perform
"The Old Gumbie Cat."

125

In the summer of 1990, *Miss Saigon* became front-page news alongside the economy and crisis in the Middle East. What made show business so important? Following protests from Asian members, the Actors Equity union objected to the brilliant actor Jonathan Pryce repeating on Broadway his London performance as the Eurasian Engineer in *Miss Saigon*. The union admitted that it had no right to reject an actor on racial grounds and producer Cameron Mackintosh argued that not only was this racism of another kind but that the show would employ many Asian actors and that touring companies would provide still more work for this minority group. But Equity barred Pryce anyway, and Mackintosh promptly cancelled the entire production despite its record-setting $25 million advance ticket sale. Within weeks, however, Equity reversed its position, allowing Pryce to appear in the Broadway production after all. By then, handsomely helped by all the publicity, the advance sale for *Miss Saigon* had swollen past $31 million.

But like Andrew Lloyd Webber and Tim Rice, Cameron Mackintosh was intensely aware of the deaf ear that Broadway had turned to changes in popular music. It had retained a musical comedy style that had been set in the thirties, developed in the forties and fifties, and then polished and professionalized. Popular music had long since changed, of course, but Broadway refused to admit that. How long could such a theater, however endearing, continue?

Cameron Mackintosh did not consider himself a creative producer who, like David Merrick for instance, might come up with the idea for *Fanny* or *Gypsy* and then bring together the composer, lyricist, librettist, director, and star. "I have found," he says, "that my own ideas are, at best, entertaining and rarely successful. I'm not inspired. I'm at my best when I recognize an artist's creation and feel, Now this is something that I can help shape and bring to fruition."

Between 1980 and 1991, he would help bring to fruition a series of fabulous hits including *Cats, Les Misérables, The Phantom of the Opera,* and *Miss Saigon.* These blockbuster musicals, after being first presented in London, arrived in New York with the fanfares of publicity and excitement once generated by the likes of *South Pacific* and *My Fair Lady,* thundering along the tryout road toward New York. "The expectations in London for those shows from the Americans," Mackintosh says, "were as big as the expectations now are in America for [my] shows from London. This only happens because, for whatever reasons, not even that they are better, there is some element in these shows that is absolutely irresistible to the public."

Irresistible? Three years after *Les Misérables* opened on Broadway, sold-out houses were still rising for nightly standing ovations. *Cats* was in its seventh year and *The Phantom of the Opera* remained the hottest ticket in New York, while advance sales for *Miss Saigon* surpassed $25 million a full year before the show was scheduled to open.

Yet never were such popular hits so controversial. Never did critics and theater intellectuals have so difficult a time getting a point that the public had no trouble with.

The musicals that Cameron Mackintosh was producing did not look or sound like traditional Broadway shows. They did not trade in the old song and dance. These were musicals that had been influenced by *Godspell* (about which the young Mackintosh had been "hysterical") and *Hair,* two shows that Broadway veterans had rejected as uncharacteristic and incomprehensible accidents. When Tim Rice and Andrew Lloyd Webber's *Jesus Christ Superstar* opened Broadway's doors to the British, it was directed by Tom O'Horgan, who had staged *Hair.* The Webber-Rice musical convinced two skeptical young Frenchmen that as songwriters they had something to give Broadway after all: They were Claude-Michel Schönberg and Alain Boublil, the authors-to-be of *Les Misérables.*

And so the invasion of Broadway was not an alien takeover at all but the work of a fresh young generation of musical devotees who, because European, were free from the constraints of habit and tradition, young artists still unspoiled enough, naive, and enthusiastic enough to bring life to this musical theater that they had dreamed about for so long.

In 1980, Andrew Lloyd Webber gave the 32-year-old Cameron Mackintosh the opportunity of a lifetime, the chance to produce *Cats*. Mackintosh was, as he put it himself, "the up-and-coming lad." He'd had a success presenting *Side by Side by Sondheim*, which was subsequently produced in New York. He had presented an "almost," *The Card*, which he considered "very nearly an American musical" and that was high praise from him indeed. "It had balls and vitality," he said. It also had a contemporary sound, strongly influenced by Burt Bachrach's *Promises, Promises*, which had challenged Broadway conventions in the late '60s with the rhythms and electronics of popular recordings.

The truth, however, was that few other producers were interested in *Cats* for, notwithstanding the successes of Webber's *Jesus Christ Superstar* and *Evita*, this show based on poems by T. S. Eliot—a show that Mackintosh himself derided as "this musical about pussycats"—was an *embarrassing* idea. Fortunately, however, Mackintosh finally grasped the theatrical possibilities that Webber already imagined and began to raise the $1 million that the production was going to cost. It was a process that would not end until the day before the premiere.

When, at the intermission (or "interval") on that London opening night, a drunk in the gallery shouted "Rubbish!" Webber and Mackintosh were both certain that they had a disaster. Then there was a bomb scare that forced the actors to skip the curtain calls; but by morning, David Merrick was offering Mackintosh the British rights to *42nd Street* in exchange for the American rights to *Cats*. The younger producer did not hesitate. "No thank you," he murmured with a smile. By 1991, *42nd Street* had earned some $10 million while *Cats was past the $100-million mark*, the most profitable show in history, with no end in sight.

Although *Cats* is the most radical of the Mackintosh-produced musicals, *Les Misérables* is the most surprising, for it has the fewest elements of musical theater. In fact, it was originally created as what the French call a "tableau," a series of still pictures illustrating a story told by a narrator and produced in a large arena. Such theater is traditional in France, where the immobile works of Racine are the classic national drama. But this is not in the nature of Broadway shows. Moreover, the French are notoriously hostile to American-style musicals, which, when they are chanced in Paris, frequently are performed to *taped orchestras*. That exemplifies the French approach, and so, had *Les Misérables* not been recorded, it probably would have been forgotten, for it ran a limited engagement of three months in Paris.

When Mackintosh was given the album by a friend, it excited him enough to contact the authors and—since Alain Boublil was still refining his English—arrange for a translation. Alan Jay Lerner, the brilliant author of *My Fair Lady*, was living in London at the time (1980) and had become the center of a salon for young Englishmen smitten by American musicals. Mackintosh had produced a successful revival of *My Fair Lady* that Lerner himself had directed, and it was Lerner he first asked to write the *Les Misérables* English adaptation. "It's a great show," the American said after hearing the album, "but I'm not right for it. I only write about people's dreams. These are real-life people. But you must pursue it."

And so Mackintosh turned to the London *Daily Express* drama critic Herbert Kretzmer, who doubled as a lyric writer for the *chanseur* Charles Aznavour. Between Boublil and Kretzmer's lyrics, *Les Misérables* would set the high-water literary mark

Cameron Mackintosh

127

for these new musicals, unless one counts the actual T. S. Eliot poems in *Cats*. (The Tony Award people would, actually giving the prize to the dead poet as not only the best lyricist of 1983 but as the best *librettist*—for a show that had no dialogue whatsoever.)

After Trevor Nunn, the artistic director of the Royal Shakespeare Company, agreed to stage *Les Misérables*, Mackintosh contrived its premiere at the RSC's Barbican Centre, hoping that, like *Nicholas Nickleby*, it would catapult from there to commercial success. But the musical was abused by the critics, many referring to it as "the miserable musical." Audiences, however, were ecstatic, and by the time *Les Miz* (as everyone in and out of show business called it) was transferred to the Palace Theatre in London's West End, it was a hit, going on to become one of the great successes of modern theatrical times. Indeed, on Broadway, after it won the 1987 Tony Award, its advance ticket sales passed the million-dollar mark and continued to grow. Three years later, the advance sale was close to *three* million dollars.

What is it about *Les Miz* that, from New York to London and from Melbourne to Tokyo, audiences find so enthralling? To a great extent, the show remains a tableau, with few dramatized scenes. Most of its songs are sung straight to the audience, and the story is played out like pictures in a storybook. A plot synopsis in the program for the English-language production does not exactly betoken an easy-

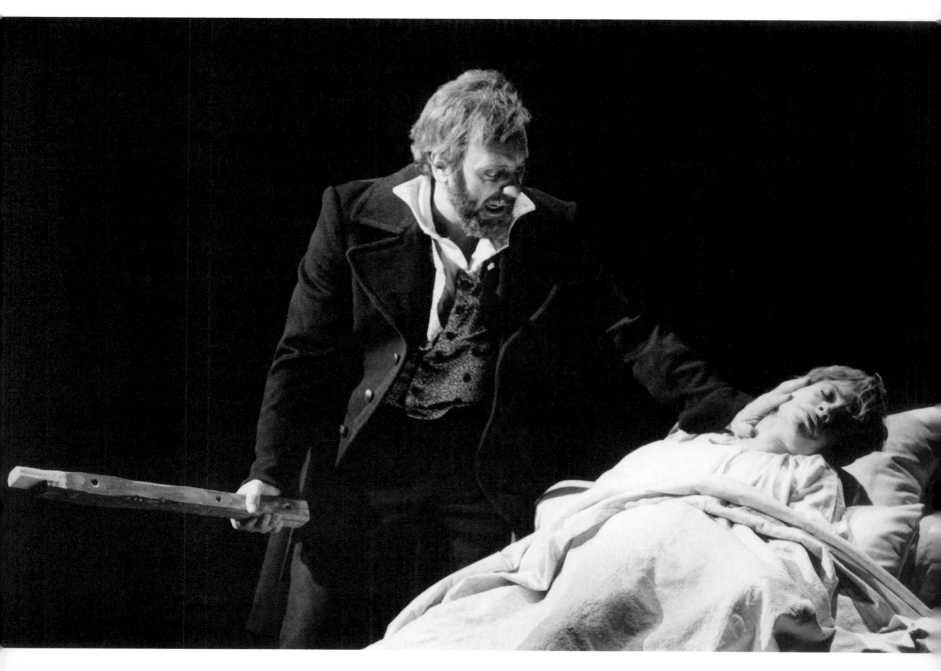

In London *Les Misérables* starred Colin Wilkinson as Valjean and Patti LuPone as Fantine.

Opposite, below: Michael Ball and Frances Ruffelle appeared in the original production of *Les Misérables* at the Barbican Centre in London, normally used by the Royal Shakespeare Company. Local critics were irked by the use of the prestigious hall for a lowly musical but audiences stormed the doors.

to-follow narrative. Moreover, there is virtually no movement in the show other than the occasionally waved banner and, here and there, a valiant march of the ensemble toward the audience.

But the varied and melodious score for this entirely sung musical never fails to thrill audiences, and there are invariably sniffles at the finale, with the survival of Jean Valjean after his imprisonment of nineteen years for stealing a loaf of bread and after a lifetime of pursuit by the detective Javert.

The Alain Boublil–Claude-Michel Schönberg songs are an odd and diverse mix, many of them stirring marches in the "Marseillaise" tradition, others heart-broken ballads that might have been written for Edith Piaf, and an occasional ensemble number that sounds Cockney enough to have come from *Oliver!*. Many of the most popular songs were written for the London production, the angry "Dog Eat Dog," for instance, the haunting "Empty Chairs at Empty Tables," and the rousing "Master of the House."

In this music, in the warmth of its sensibility, and in its open emotionalism lies the show's appeal. Like the Andrew Lloyd Webber approach that inspired it, *Les Misérables* brings to the public a musical theater in keeping with contemporary times rather than the old Broadway razzmatazz that can seem gaudy, shallow, and corny to modern audiences. *Les Misérables* has size and muscle, it deals in passionate feelings; it sings out, and the songs have a contemporary feel even though they are hardly rock-and-roll as today's youngsters understand it. Moreover the orchestra is only mildly electrified. But most important, the approach of the show is not cynical or smart-aleck like old Broadway. It is honest and heartfelt, and that is appealing to audiences.

Why hadn't Broadway professionals been able to do this? They were blinded by tradition, by the love of Cole Porter and Frank Loesser and Rodgers and Hammerstein, as if one kind of musical theater precluded all others.

For *Cats*, his first major American production, Mackintosh had allied himself with the powerful Shubert Organization, New York's biggest theater owner and producer, taking advantage of its expertise and financial clout (there would be no small investors). In return, he was invited to co-produce *The Little Shop of Horrors*. This very funny and unique show based on the cult classic horror movie became a great success and Mackintosh himself presented the British version for a two-year run.

Jean Valjean (Colin Wilkinson) confronts his detective nemesis, Javert (Roger Allain), in *Les Misérables*.

One reason for the wide appeal of *Les Miz* is its frank emotionalism — visually, thematically, and musically. "But the end of 1992, I believe there will be thirty productions of *Les Miz*," Mackintosh said. "No show in history has had that."

Right:
Resembling numbers in *Oliver!*, the song from *Les Misérables* "Master of the House" sounds joyous and lusty as a corner pub.

Meantime, on *Les Misérables*'s opening night in London, its authors confided that they were starting work on a new show. So, following in the steps of Andrew Lloyd Webber, they were taking creative charge. And also like Webber, who had inspired them, Boublil and Schönberg were setting every word of dialogue to music, virtually ruling out any substantial changes in their conception. This did not mean an end to other kinds of musicals, but it did mean an emergence of composers as dramatists. It was a re-assertion of authors' creative rights after a long period of domination by directors.

Not until May, 1986, did Mackintosh learn what his *Les Miz* authors were up to. They appeared at his London office with a synopsis of the first act of *Miss Saigon* and a tape recording of its music. After listening to these materials, Mackintosh was convinced that Boublil and Schönberg were "the best musical dramatists since Rodgers and Hammerstein. Webber," he admits, "is more showmanly. He has a great sense of theater. But he isn't essentially a dramatist."

It is an opinion to be respected, but a certain amount of skepticism would be wise, as Mackintosh and Webber went separate ways after *The Phantom of the Opera*.

Although Alain Boublil's mastery of the English language was now all but complete, for insurance Mackintosh engaged one of the most talented of Broadway's lyricists to help with the *Miss Saigon* libretto. This was Richard Maltby, Jr., who had polished the lyrics for *Tell Me on a Sunday* (the "Song" in Webber's *Song and Dance*). A truly brilliant lyricist, Maltby was also a successful director *(Ain't Misbehavin', Song and Dance, Baby)*, and his theatricality, his sense of Broadway, and his keen awareness of American taste would be further assets. Moreover he was young enough and smart enough to be open to this new kind of musical theater that Webber and Rice, and now Boublil and Schönberg, were developing. Indeed, Maltby believed that these through-composed shows were "re-inventing the form."

By the time that *Miss Saigon* had its world premiere (the autumn of 1989), London audiences were so familiar with and excited by this re-invented form of musical that, months away, they could sense a successful one heading their way, much as New York audiences had once looked forward to a Rodgers and Hammerstein blockbuster. These premonitions seemed *never* to be mistaken. Audiences just weren't fooled by the inevitable attempts in London to copy the big Andrew Lloyd Webber and Boublil-Schönberg musicals—spectacular, entirely sung shows like *Time*, *Metropolis*, *Carrie*, and *Chess*. Only the last show succeeded at all and that because Tim Rice's name was on the libretto (and because, more to the point, it was simply better than the others, although still not quite good enough).

Like all traditional smash hits, then, *Miss Saigon* built up an exhilarating head of steam as it roared down the road toward its premiere, billowing with assurance. The Cameron Mackintosh imprimatur itself had become a kind of guarantee of good showmanship. And audiences were faithful; *Miss Saigon* had been written by the authors of their beloved *Les Misérables*. Thus it was a hit before it even opened at the Theatre Royal Drury Lane.

Miss Saigon is not another *Les Misérables*. In some ways it is more theatrical, in other ways more conventional. Its story is hardly a match for the Victor Hugo classic, but what both shows do share is the lyricism, the sincerity of emotion, and the drive of the Boublil-Schönberg musical scores, as well as an excitement and muscle of staging notion. *Miss Saigon* generates these forceful qualities from the opening whir of the helicopter rotor that begins the overture and that becomes a recurring motif throughout the show, culminating in the famous onstage landing of an apparently real helicopter.

As a Vietnam War version of the *Phantom of the Opera*'s famous falling chandelier, the descending "helicopter" is only one of several incidents in *Miss Saigon* reminiscent of other shows. Bob Avian (Michael Bennett's co-choreographer for *A Chorus Line*), for instance, obviously remembered "Hey, Big Spender" from *Sweet Charity* when he created a dance for the Saigon prostitutes, and director Nicholas Hytner seems to have been all too aware of the Joel Grey Master of Ceremonies in *Cabaret* when he staged the character of The Engineer. This central figure is both a real character—a pimp and wartime profiteer—as well as an unreal, cynical Greek Chorus. There are also resonances of *Evita* in the show's giant pictures and banners dropping from above, and in scenery that pulls away to leave the stage empty.

Co-authors of *Les Misérables* and *Miss Saigon* Claude-Michel Schönberg *(left)* and Alain Boublil.

But showmen have traditionally been influenced by (all right, have stolen from) their colleagues. The theater, after all, is a temple of deception with an appropriately slippery code of ethics. Given its playful purposes, theft is a minor crime. All that counts is whether a show entertains once the curtain has risen.

Miss Saigon opens in a GI bar in wartime Vietnam. It is 1973, and the story will be a broad version of *Madame Butterfly*. Pinkerton has become Chris, an American marine, and Butterfly is an inexperienced young prostitute, Kim. She is among the girls rounded up by the hustling Engineer, who starts the story by staging a "Miss Saigon" contest in the bar to promote his whores.

> The heat is on in Saigon
> The girls are hotter 'n hell
> One of these slits here
> Will be Miss Saigon
> God, the tension is high
> Not to mention the smell

The girls fantasize about snaring one of these boys and escaping to America, a place they can imagine only from what they have seen in the movies. In contrast to the rocking number that just ended, this music is exquisitely melodic, slow, and dreamy.

> The movie in my mind
> The dream they leave behind
> A scene I can't erase
> And in a strong GI's embrace
> Flee this life, flee this place

135

Miss Saigon opens in a GI bar in Vietnam with the number "The Heat Is on in Saigon." The character called Engineer, a pimp, has organized a beauty contest to promote his prostitutes.

Jonathan Pryce perches upon a Cadillac at the climax of *Miss Saigon*. Despite trepidation about this sardonic "American Dream" number, it was kept intact for the Broadway version.

Momentarily the corner of a small bedroom rolls on stage (the kind of set, a "trolley," that was typical in the 1950s). Chris and Kim are already in love — this is not sophisticated storytelling — and not long afterward Chris is sent home while Kim has his child and then moves on with the Engineer, first to Hanoi and then to Bangkok, notorious for its sex marts. The stage explodes into a gaudy erotic carnival, horrifying and magnetic, with prostitutes writhing in cages. The Engineer, wise and stupid, sophisticated and childish, a manipulator and a victim, derides the girls' (and his own) fantasy of America. A full-sized, tail-finned Cadillac rolls to the center for this sardonic vaudeville, "The American Dream," performed as a black and sinister song and dance.

After Cameron Mackintosh successfully kept Jonathan Pryce in the American production of *Miss Saigon*, he insisted that London actress Lea Salonga repeat her co-starring role as well.

What's that I smell in the air?
    The American Dream
Sweet as a new millionaire
    The American Dream
Pre-packed and ready-to-wear
    My American Dream
Fat like a chocolate eclair
    As I suck out the cream

Luck by the tail
How can I fail?
And best of all it's for sale

The American Dream

Not all the London critics raved, but it hardly mattered. Audiences can usually be persuaded to stay away from bad shows but not in the case of one they already know they want to see. After all the negative reviews of such popular musicals as *Evita* and *Starlight Express*, West End theatergoers had good reason to distrust the critics, and *Miss Saigon* became Mackintosh's fourth blockbuster in fewer than ten years.

By the time it was ready for Broadway, *Miss Saigon* was the most expensive ($10 million) show in history, with the highest-priced tickets ($100 for the best seats in the house).

Not that many years earlier, Broadway had been only a dream to Cameron Mackintosh, a youngster dressed up in a neatly pressed kilt, taken by his parents to see the London musical *Salad Days*. And not that many years earlier, Mackintosh had postponed a major business appointment rather than delay a chance to visit New York and actually see a Broadway musical for the first time in his life.

"I'm doing what I'm doing," he says now, "because I love it. I'm not doing it for the money and as a result, I have more money than I can ever dream of."

CHAPTER
8
SHOW MUSIC

The first generation of Broadway composers—the artists who originated the basic style, sound, and tradition of musical comedy—was dominated by the *Giants* of our musical stage. These were Jerome Kern, who more or less invented the modern popular song and could be considered the father of Broadway musicals; Irving Berlin, the supreme writer of popular songs; Richard Rodgers, our finest melodist and probably the greatest natural talent in Broadway musical history; Cole Porter, who wrote our most literate, sophisticated, and civilized songs; as well as George Gershwin, who personified not only Broadway but America in all its youthful vigor, promise, and confidence.

There were, of course, other gifted composers and lyricists in those early, halcyon years of Broadway musicals. In the book *Broadway Musicals* they were called the *Masters* and included such songwriters as Vincent Youmans, Arthur Schwartz, Harold Arlen, Vernon Duke, Noël Coward, Hugh Martin, Burton Lane, Kurt Weill, Frank Loesser, Jule Styne, and Frederick Loewe—they wrote from the 1920s into the 1950s and provided us with our repertory of beloved musicals and songs that have become an American cultural treasure.

In the process, librettos were refined. The featherweight musical comedies of the early days gave way to Oscar Hammerstein II's infinitely better-crafted musical plays, from *Show Boat* to *Oklahoma!* and *The King and I*, and it became apparent that the script of a musical—its "book"—had to provide the architecture on which to hang all the wonderful musical numbers. Without that, even the loveliest of songs would flail and collapse.

The following generation of Broadway songwriters, our *Professionals*, maintained the tradition of composer-lyricist partnerships: Richard Adler and Jerry Ross, John Kander and Fred Ebb, Jerry Bock and Sheldon Harnick, Lee Adams and Charles Strouse, Tom Jones and Harvey Schmidt. Composers who wrote their own lyrics, such as Jerry Herman or Stephen Sondheim, became the exception. And these *Professionals* created the shows that established musicals as the dominating theater of Broadway.

Tyne Daly helped make the 1989 revival of *Gypsy* a success. The Jule Styne-Stephen Sondheim score meantime reasserted its theatrical electricity, its unity, its enduring greatness. By decade's end, Styne had become the dean of establishment Broadway composers.

Yet only a few of them were able to change with the economics and tastes of the 1980s. The most adaptable among them was Cy Coleman, one of the most facile, gifted, and productive composers in modern Broadway history.

Born in 1929, Coleman was a child prodigy, trained as a classical pianist. He was in love with popular music, however, selling songs by the time he was sixteen, ultimately teaming up with a bright young lyricist, Carolyn Leigh, to write such sophisticated hits as "The Best Is Yet to Come" and "Witchcraft." Turning to the musical theater, traditionally the medium for superior popular music, Coleman and Leigh wrote the successful 1960 Lucille Ball vehicle *Wildcat* (with its hit song "Hey, Look Me Over") and followed it up, two years later, with one of Broadway's funniest shows, Neil Simon's *Little Me*, starring Sid Caesar.

But Carolyn Leigh was as difficult as she was brilliant (she would die tragically young), and Coleman turned to the great lyricist Dorothy Fields for his next shows, *Sweet Charity* and *Seesaw*. He would never again have a regular collaborator. But as a prodigiously gifted composer, his brains, humor, and vivacity would lend vast charm to his inventive music. And with each different show, his collaborators would be suited to the musical and theatrical style at hand.

For instance, the 1978 *On the Twentieth Century* was a mock operetta and throughout their careers, Betty Comden and Adolph Green had been attached to classical music. Had not their first Broadway show, *On the Town*, been written with Leonard Bernstein? They were perfectly suited to collaborate with Coleman, and the team was mutually inspirational, the satire in the lyrics and the satire in the music

Above and opposite: Composer Cy Coleman himself produced *Barnum* and demonstrated how a smaller show could still have the feel of a big Broadway musical. The circus atmosphere of *Barnum* was ingeniously depicted.

141

Glenn Close sang beautifully in *Barnum*, here with the charming star, Jim Dale, before going on to dramatic stardom in Hollywood.

urging each other to giddier heights. This was a truly precocious score, and its music showed how exhilarating the combination of classical training and theatrical sense could be. While there have been other Broadway composers with the self-same combination (Charles Strouse and, of course, Bernstein himself), Cy Coleman seems to take unique pleasure in exercising his extraordinary gifts as if, quite innocently, he cannot himself believe that a single composer can be so talented.

He had demonstrated even before *Twentieth Century* — with the four-character *I Love My Wife* — that smaller shows were viable on Broadway. In 1980, his *Barnum* was not quite that small, but it had only one set and it had no chorus of singers or dancers. What it did have, however, was a Broadway sound in the orchestra pit and a Broadway flash on stage. This show felt full-sized, and in accomplishing that, Cy Coleman made a case for the modestly produced musical (in fact co-producing *Barnum* himself).

Throughout the 1980s, Broadway would debate the possibilities of smaller shows, the consensus being that audiences who pay a great deal for tickets want to see their money's worth on stage. Perhaps there was some truth in this dismaying view, for even those smaller shows that were well received (*Romance, Romance*, for instance, or *Baby*) did not become hits.

But since there was as yet no small Broadway musical that had opened to rave reviews there was no reason to conclude that only big musicals could succeed in big Broadway theaters. Coleman's *Barnum*, while no blockbuster hit, certainly demonstrated that a modestly produced musical could attract two years' worth of audiences, and that wasn't bad for a small show.

Barnum's star was Jim Dale, one of the few contemporary performers who could be called a star in the old-fashioned sense. These past decades have not been kind to performers. Rather, today's stars have been the choreographer-directors, or composers like Andrew Lloyd Webber, or the shows themselves. For certain, the era of the Ethel Mermans and Mary Martins, the Robert Prestons, Yul Brynners, and Rex Harrisons — those days were past.

And yet, and yet. When an actor is irresistible, the public will embrace him, and Jim Dale was irresistible as Phineas T. Barnum. He was a performer who played bigger than life, so engaging that when (some years later) the British actor Robert Lindsay won audiences' hearts starring in *Me and My Girl*, Dale could replace him and steal those same hearts away. Thus it was that in *Barnum* he magnetized theatergoers and ruled the stage. (His leading lady, then an unknown, was Glenn Close.)

Cy Coleman's collaborators on *Barnum* were a very experienced librettist, Michael Stewart (author of *Bye Bye Birdie* and *Hello, Dolly!*), who wrote not the libretto but the lyrics, and a very inexperienced librettist, Mark Bramble, who unfortunately did write it. However Coleman himself is a funny and spirited fellow, and it was his exuberance that seemed to energize the show. The excitement was generated as the curtain was lighted up for his "Overture Chase," after which Dale stepped forth to greet the audience.

Barnum's the name, P. T. Barnum. And I want
to tell you that tonight you are going to see —

142

bar none—every sight, wonder and miracle
that name stands for!

And then, from the high-spirited tomfoolery of circus orchestrations to the richness of Coleman's ballad "The Colors of My Life," *Barnum* played to music steeped in Broadway juices. Yet, because of the composer's special combination of talents, the score was musicianly as well as catchy and theatrical.

But the next years were frustrating ones for him as one show *(Home Again, Home Again)* was aborted on the road and another—*Welcome to the Club*—was a disaster in plain view on Broadway. That musical proved once again that there are certain ideas gilt-edged in hopelessness. This one was for a musical comedy about alimony jail.

Like many Broadway composers, Cy Coleman works on several projects at once because there are so many variables, from financing to the availability of prominent directors, and of course some projects ripen more quickly than others. For instance, while he was writing the music for *The Will Rogers Follies*, with a book by Peter Stone and lyrics by Betty Comden and Adolph Green, to be directed by

Cy Coleman wrote the music for Welcome to the Club, which starred Marilyn Sokol and Avery Schreiber.

143

City of Angels uses an ingenious production scheme: the left side of the stage, representing "real life," appears in full color; at right, in black and white, is the "movie version" written by the hero. Here, at left, the screenwriter's secretary sings. At right, the character inspired by the secretary sings with her.

Tommy Tune, he was also working on *The Life* with lyricist Ira Gasman, and *City of Angels* with David Zippel's lyrics, its libretto by Larry Gelbart. The latter show, as it turned out, was the first to be produced, and became the first Tony Award winner for best musical of the 1990s.

At first, this idea might have seemed poor, or at least tired—a satire of Raymond Chandler–style Hollywood detective movies of the 1940s. But some ideas can be made to work through imagination (*The Pajama Game*, for instance, a musical about union problems in a pajama factory). *City of Angels* became a wonderful show and a considerable hit because of the way in which it proved out a fundamental rule of the musical stage: the most important element in any musical is its book. As written and as it played on stage Larry Gelbart's script was the smoothest, most ingenious, and funniest to come along in many years. Broadway musicals had started out life as musical comedy. In an effort at dignity, Oscar Hammerstein II promoted sobriety in his musical plays. Ever since, much of the laughter had gone out of musicals, and it was rare that one of them was actually funny. Gelbart had cowritten (with Burt Shevelove) perhaps the wittiest of all, *A Funny Thing Happened on the Way to the Forum*. This new show of his, *City of Angels*, may have been the funniest since.

Gelbart's notion could not have been fresher. An idealistic writer is lured to Hollywood for the screen adaptation of his detective novel. The studio chief proclaims admiration for the author and respect for a writer's independence while

undermining, corrupting, and rewriting every word of the script. ("The book may be yours but trust me, the movie is mine!") With each change, the script-in-progress is enacted alongside the real-life events. Most of the characters are played by actors doubling in roles — for the writer's real life finds its way into the movie and he himself develops a relationship with his alter ego, the tough-talking and cynical detective hero.

Audiences often wonder what directors do, exactly. For this show, Michael Blakemore decided to have the real-life scenes done in full-color, that is, the events in the Hollywood studio involving the actors, the writer, his wife, his girlfriend, the studio chief, and the rest. On the other side of the stage, entirely in black-and-white, the movie is played out as it is being written and made. These costumes and scenery are all done in the style of a 1940s black-and-white movie.

Not only did this make for a comic visual situation but helped to clarify what might have been a clever but confusing script.

City of Angels came as a relief after decades of not very funny musical theater. Unfortunately, however, this show never seems musical. Few of its songs are musically staged, and fewer still cry out to be staged. In fact, many are sung in a radio studio by "The Angel City 4," a pop singing group. Exactly what they or their songs have to do with the show is never clear.

The finale of *City of Angels* provides "a real Hollywood ending," as one of the characters requests.

THE BOOK

CITY OF ANGELS

Of a musical's basic ele-
ments — the book, music,
and lyrics — the book is the
most important because it
provides a style, a reason,
and most important
of all, a structure for the
production. This spine
keeps the musical numbers
from collapsing.

Larry Gelbart's libretto
for *City of Angels* is a
model of precision, lean-
ness, and dry comedy
while being at the same
time ingenious. It is
perhaps the funniest
script for a musical since
Gelbart's own *A Funny
Thing Happened on the
Way to the Forum*,
written with Burt
Shevelove.

In this scene, Gelbart
leads into a Cy Coleman–
David Zippel song that
showcases the shameless
corruption of the movie
producer, Buddy Fidler,
in dealing with the
hero-writer, Stine.

Opposite:
James Naughton played
the movie detective, Stone,
in *City of Angels* and Dee
Hoty was the *femme fatale*
who hires him.

ACT ONE
Scene Eight

BUDDY'S Office

BUDDY, having a haircut, is reading screenplay pages aloud to GILBERT,
his barber

BUDDY
". . . somehow I was getting the idea that this was God's way of punishing me for
having a hundred dollars all at once."

GILBERT
Is that supposed to be funny?

BUDDY
Half-and-half.

GILBERT
It's about right, then.

BUDDY
Donna! Waiting is expensive.

(BUDDY'S secretary enters)

DONNA
He's on his way.

BUDDY
Here would be even better. That dress is half-an-inch too long. It'll photograph
even longer.

BUDDY

No, no, no. There're too many words now. Give me pictures. Paint me scenes. Movies are shadows. They're light, they're dark. They're faces ten feet high. Close-up of him! Close-up of her! Cut to close-up of husband watching close-up of her watching close-up of him!
(Beat)
You'll get it, you'll see. Sweetheart, nobody gets a hole-in-one their first time at bat. There's people make a fortune writing movies, and *they* don't know how. I mean, no offense, everybody and his brother write books, but a screenplay . . .

STINE

That's a ballgame of a different color, right?

BUDDY

When Buddy Fidler talks, you're not listening to someone else.
(Sings)
I'VE GOT TWELVE NOMINATIONS A HALF DOZEN OSCARS
NINE CARS AND THREE EX-WIVES TO SHOW
THAT IN THIS BUSINESS OF REFUSE AND NEPHEWS I KNOW MY
   STUFF

YOU'RE A LITERARY GREAT
WHO SHOULD OF WON A PULITZER PRIZE
I WOULD NEVER CANNIBALIZE
OR IMPAIR A SINGLE HAIR OR PHRASE
OF YOUR AMAZING OPUS
   (etc.)

DONNA

I'm not in a movie.

BUDDY

Everybody's in a movie. Sometimes we just turn the camera on.
(Looking at pages)
You can tell a writer every time. Words, words, words, that's all they know. This could take awhile. Who've I got for lunch?

DONNA

Carla.

BUDDY

(Engrossed in pages)
Who?

DONNA

Your wife.

BUDDY

Cancel her.

DONNA

One or two dozen?

BUDDY
Whichever's more.
          (Looking in mirror)
Beautiful. The man's an artist.
          (To GILBERT,
          affectionately)
Took me long enough to teach you.

GILBERT
See you tomorrow, Mr. Fidler.

          (HE exits, as STINE enters)

STINE
Knock, knock?

BUDDY
The man of my dreams. I just got the pages where Stone gets beat up.

STINE
You like 'em?

BUDDY
Like is for pishers. These are to love. They're perfect.
          (Laughs)
But we'll fix 'em.

STINE
Can't I finish the script before we fix it?

BUDDY
Sure, you can finish it, but first, we'll fix.

STINE
What is it, you want new words?

Selling screenwriter Gregg Edelman a bill of goods, René Auberjonois (left) created the hilarious role of the egotistical movie producer, Buddy Fidler, in City of Angels. Auberjonois is one of the finest classical actors Broadway has ever produced, but classics do not make for American theater fame. He is best known to the public for the television series Benson.

149

One of the reasons why *City of Angels* often seemed less of a musical and more of a comedy was that many of the songs were sung on a "radio program."

Overall, *City of Angels* shows Cy Coleman reveling in his choice of musical style, the jazz-influenced popular music of the 1940s. Musical satire is difficult to sustain over the duration of a show, although it has been done before by Stephen Sondheim *(Follies)*, Leonard Bernstein *(Candide)*, John Kander *(Chicago)*, and Coleman himself *(On the Twentieth Century)*. The difference between those shows and *City of Angels* is that they satirized various kinds of *theater* music while popular jazz singing of the 1940s was designed to be heard on the radio or records, not seen or staged. Coleman's score glows with knowledgeability of this kind of music, yet the songs that are *not* sung by "The Angel City 4" but by characters in the story are much more effective. They suggest what Coleman might have had in mind — to set music of the era to the purposes of the story at hand. When he succeeds, the idea's possibilities are apparent, as in "You Can Always Count on Me," a typical 1940s list song, a series of examples — in this case of a woman being victimized.

> I've been the "other woman" since my puberty began
> I crashed the junior prom
> And met the only married man

Lyricist David Zippel wrote especially appropriate words for another number, sung by the amusingly corrupt movie producer Buddy Fidler. It works as musical theater as the producer tells the hero-novelist Stine about the Hollywood facts of life:

> You wouldn't want to upset Buddy
> This is advice, not a threat, buddy,

But see how tough things can get, buddy
When things get tough it can get bloody
Baby, nobody says no, buddy

Such clever, "feminine" rhymes (rhyming before the final syllable) as "upset Buddy," "threat, buddy," and "get, buddy" are also smoothly wrought to suit the character's personality and match the libretto's style of humor. Zippel occasionally makes a young man's mistake of showing off with lyrics so clever they seem contrived and are sometimes too dense:

And come to think of it
Your writing always mirrors our relationship
With dangers cropping up
And sweet young strangers popping up like weeds

So if you wish official pardoning
You'd better do a little gardening
Ya know ya needn't be so gen'rous with your seeds
Your fertile lies don't fertilize
It needs work

You had to ruin it
This plot has got a lot of

Cy Coleman and David Zippel wrote the mock torch song "With Every Breath I Take" for Kay McClelland to sing in *City of Angels*.

Déjà vu in it — familiarity
And in this case we both know
What that breeds

Such trickery — the gardening metaphor extended to sexual seeds, or lines like "fertile lies don't fertilize," and rhymes like "ruin it" and "déjà vu in it" — is probably beyond exhilaration and nearer self-consciousness. Elsewhere in *City of Angels*, Zippel's lyrics are more relaxed, in keeping with Cy Coleman's professionalism. In a duet between the novelist Stine and his detective Stone, Coleman and Zippel collaborate perfectly as the music suits the show's level of satire while the lyrics deftly elaborate on the relationship between novelist and character.

STINE
Just what you are I'll spell out
You are a novel pain
One speck of lint that fell out
The last time that I picked by brain

STONE
You are so jealous of my track record
Tolstoy do tell us your feeble hack record

BOTH
You're nothing without me
A no one who'd go undefined
You wouldn't exist
You'd never be missed

STINE
I tell you you're out of my mind

This is clever work on the parts of both the lyricist and the composer, but Coleman has long since proved himself clever. When he is serious he can also be wonderful. An ironic, quasi-bolero titled "Funny" yanks all emotional plugs and lets the novelist cry out. The piece works and is ultimately thrilling. At the end, however, *City of Angels* still seems more a comedy with songs than a comic musical. Perhaps Coleman had too great a say about the show's music. Perhaps Michael Blakemore, directing his first Broadway musical, was relieved to be relieved of musical responsibilities, but it is not wise to give a composer such leeway. Too often, decisions are ruled by musical interests rather than those of the overall production. In this case, the lyrics generally seem more basic to *City of Angels* than does the music.

Coleman's theatrical future, like his past, is difficult to predict because every show of his is so different. That is admirable, for a theater score should be inspired by and tailored to the material at hand, its purpose and production style. But in Coleman's case, musical facility seems equally the reason for the differences between *Little Me* (witty, very *Broadway* music), *Seesaw* (melodic but untheatrical songs, more like popular music), *On the Twentieth Century* (a mock operetta composed with dazzling élan), and *City of Angels* (1940s-style vocal jazz). His following show, 1991's exhilarating *The Will Rogers Follies*, found Coleman reverting to a Broadway style that was all but gone from Broadway. And the restoration was delicious.

Coleman's gifts are almost scary. He has been known to compose on the instant, in plain view of his gulping lyricists, which is something Richard Rodgers

alone was celebrated for. Among Broadway's composers over the past few decades, only Leonard Bernstein was his superior as a pianist. But at the age of sixty (in 1991), he still seemed to be a prodigy. He had written some of Broadway's most ingratiating scores, but because music comes so easily to him, he had not yet made the greatest demands on his talent. A theater score drawing on every Cy Coleman resource at the highest state of development is something not merely to hope for but to anticipate with awe.

In a similar way that couldn't be more different, Jerry Herman is also a natural, certainly the great melodist on modern Broadway. But concluding the 1970s with the worst flop of his career, the 61-performance *Grand Tour*, he was sunk in a professional depression. He had no doubt been spoiled by the stunning series of hits

Tommy Tune became Broadway's reigning choreographer-director during the 1980s. While the big British shows were being spectacular with chandeliers and helicopters, Tune — when he chose to be spectacular — was pure Broadway, as shown in *The Will Rogers Follies*, which opened in April 1991.

153

with which he had begun his career — *Milk and Honey, Hello, Dolly!,* and *Mame.* He was not prepared for ten years of failures and was pained most of all by the quick closing of *Mack and Mabel,* which he justifiably considered his best score.

Could Herman work out this career crisis? His kind of shows and his kind of show tunes were beginning to sound old-fashioned, even in the forgiving atmosphere of a Broadway theater. Yet he came up with his biggest hit of all, one of the few American shows to achieve a blockbuster success in the 1980s, and that was *La Cage aux Folles* in 1983.

It drew on an unlikely source, the French film of the same title, a love story about a homosexual couple operating a transvestite night club, and the complications that arise when the son of one of them marries into a moralistic bourgeois family.

Broadway audiences also tend to be moralistic, narrow-minded, and bourgeois, especially regarding musical theater, which is generally looked upon as family entertainment. A lavish show about a homosexual marriage, with transvestite production numbers, hardly seemed a prime candidate as family fare, but the director of this musical was the wise and sophisticated Broadway veteran Arthur Laurents, who had done the librettos for both *West Side Story* and *Gypsy.* The libretto for *La Cage aux Folles* was being written by Harvey Fierstein, who had enjoyed a tremendous success with his play *Torch Song Trilogy,* a tender story of a transvestite, his mother, and his paternal relationship with a youth. If audiences embraced that play, why not a musical on the subject?

Laurents took a cautious approach to the risky materials. Broadway musicals are about hits, they are not for the championship of causes. He knew that audiences could go only so far in dealing with homosexuals in a love story. A crucial element of the plot was for one of the couple of homosexual lovers to be plainly "normal," or masculine-acting, and a crucial element of the casting would be for that character to be played by an unassailably manly actor. Only then could the other lover be contrastingly, and acceptably, effeminate or campy. However, Laurents was also willing to indulge the show in lavish transvestite production numbers. He could trust audiences with that because there is a long history of conventional audiences enjoying drag shows.

The director drew the line, however, at any display of physical affection. "One kiss between these guys," he said, "and half the house would have walked out." He was not directing a Broadway musical to give lessons in sexual sociology and not in the business of embarrassing theatergoers. And his approach succeeded. *La Cage aux Folles* became simply a musical about entertainment and humanity.

The Harvey Fierstein book and Jerry Herman's songs were true to this goal of storytelling, warmth, and glitter. *La Cage aux Folles* was hardly an adventurous musical in any sense except its subject matter. It was a traditional book musical with its numbers spotted at the traditional points. Jerry Herman's songs were in the full-throated vernacular of conservative Broadway, and his lyrics were likewise straightforward.

> The best of times is now
> What's left of summer but a faded rose?
> The best of times is now
> As for tomorrow, well, who knows? Who knows? Who knows?
>
> So hold this moment fast
> And live and love as hard as you know how
> And make this moment last
> Because the best of times is now, is now, is now

However much as *La Cage aux Folles* looked and acted like a traditional Broadway musical, its subject was, after all, homosexual love. The signature for many Jerry Herman shows, since *Hello, Dolly!*, has been a crowning anthem of identity. *Mame* had its title song, while *Mack and Mabel* had "When Mabel Comes in the Room." "The Best of Times" was but one of two such songs in this show, and befitting the subject, the other rousing anthem was more than a salute to an extravagant woman like Dolly or Mame. The anthem sung by the transvestite Albin is a proud and defiant proclamation of self.

> I am what I am
> I am my own special creation
> So, come take a look
> Give me the hook or the ovation
>
> It's my world that I want
> To have a little pride in
> My world and
> It's not a place I have to hide in

Overleaf:
Before staging The *Will Rogers Follies* in the spring of 1991, Tommy Tune was accused of avoiding the Broadway musical establishment. He seemed to seek out fresh if untested composers, lyricists, and book writers—with the exception of librettist Peter Stone, who had revised both *My One and Only* and *Grand Hotel*. However, with this show, Tune teamed up not only with Stone again but also with Broadway regulars Cy Coleman, Betty Comden, and Adolph Green. Their songs reflected both the pit band sound of a *Ziegfeld Follies* and the rural style of Will Rogers, the cowboy who, as casually as spinning his lariat, spun political satire into stage stardom.

The Will Rogers Follies showed Tune stretching the musical form once again, this time to create an abstraction of the legendary *Ziegfeld Follies*, with archetypal chorus beauties on an archetypal Follies staircase. But, as ever, this director's language was the language of Broadway—the dazzle and glitter of its musical theater, tested and stretched. Appropriately for a show about the Follies, this musical marked the re-opening of Broadway's legendary Palace Theatre after being closed several years for renovation.

Three Dolly Levis turned up in *Jerry's Girls*, a tribute to the very Broadway-sounding songs of composer Jerry Herman. The Dollys *(left to right)* are Leslie Uggams, Chita Rivera, and Dorothy Loudon.

Life's not worth a damn
Till you can say
Hey world, I am what I am

The show was one of the greatest successes of the 1980s, but because of the AIDS epidemic burgeoning in the middle of the decade, subsequent companies of *La Cage aux Folles* all but disappeared as its romantic subject became linked to the catastrophic disease.

Except for contributing several songs to *A Day in Hollywood/A Night in the Ukraine* and supervising *Jerry's Girls*, with its reprises of his most popular numbers, Herman produced no other shows during the 1980s. Sad to say, that was much the case with most of his contemporaries among the *Professionals*. These accomplished show writers who had made the 1960s and 1970s a time of musical-theater polish and abundance were unable to come to terms with changing times, seemingly unable to imagine any other kinds of musicals except the ones they'd grown up with, had been inspired by, and had themselves been writing.

Audiences, however, were no longer so regularly pleased. Charles Strouse, for instance, the gifted composer of such hits as *Bye Bye Birdie* and *Annie*, failed with *Charlie and Algernon, Dance a Little Closer, Rags, A Broadway Musical*, and *Bring Back Birdie*. The five didn't play a month's performances among them, and the sequel to *Annie, Annie 2*, closed during a Washington, D.C., tryout in 1990.

158

Similarly, during the 1980s, Harvey Schmidt and Tom Jones wrote two shows that never reached Broadway, *Colette* and *Grover's Corner*. The latter never even made it into production because Mary Martin — who was to play the Stage Manager in this musical version of *Our Town* — fell mortally ill with cancer.

John Kander and Fred Ebb, authors of *Cabaret* and *Chicago*, began the decade with *Woman of the Year*, which ran almost two years on the popularity of Lauren Bacall, and, subsequently, Raquel Welch but wasn't a very good show and did just enough business to keep open without repaying its investors. Surprisingly, Liza Minnelli, who might have been expected to be an even greater attraction than Bacall, could not do as much for a better Kander and Ebb show, *The Rink* (1984). Six years later, when the team tried to develop a musical in a suburban university theater, away from Broadway pressures, they were tracked down by critics, and even before *The Kiss of the Spider Woman* was pronounced finished by its makers, it was pronounced finished by the reviewers. Critics are supposed to champion the theater, but in this instance, they seemed more interested in the news value of a Kander and Ebb musical staged by Harold Prince than they were in respecting a work process. *The Kiss of the Spider Woman* was certainly a troubled show but also an unusual, ambitious, and promising one. It was denied a chance to find itself, and Prince was denied his effort at developing a good musical at its own pace despite the escalating economic pressures of Broadway.

At stake, then, was the very future of musicals — at least as the Broadway tradition had evolved. If the only hits were blockbuster shows, and if the mature generation of show writers could no longer find their touch, was that touch in fact no longer to be found? If there was going to be a new generation of composers, lyricists, and librettists, where was it?

Tom Jones and Harvey Schmidt, whose *Fantasticks* entered its fourth decade run in 1991, showcased Diana Rigg as *Colette* but failed to make a Broadway opening, closing on the road.

Liza Minnelli and Chita Rivera, a couple of old friends, played daughter and mother in Kander and Ebb's *The Rink*.

Although Anthony Quinn had never appeared in a Broadway musical, playing the title role in a revival of John Kander and Fred Ebb's *Zorba* (based on his movie *Zorba the Greek*) proved him to be an electrifying performer and a phenomenal box-office attraction.

Right:
Lauren Bacall starred in the musical version of the movie *Woman of the Year*. The show did not have a top-drawer score by Kander and Ebb but Bacall was attraction enough.

Graciela Daniele emerged toward the end of the 1980s offering some hope that the void left by all the lost choreographer—directors might begin filling. This is her production of *Once on This Island*.

9
GENERATION

Talent has always been the theater's most abundant (and wasted) resource. In the direst of Broadway times, when the chances for a production are slimmest, even then, young writers write musicals and young composers compose them.

The theater's upcoming writers of the 1980s accepted rock-and-roll as the popular music of the nation, turning their energies to writing for the stage. There was not going to be a merging of the two. In the recent past such gifted composer-performers as Paul McCartney, James Taylor, Paul Simon, Carole King, Neil Sedaka, Elton John, or Randy Newman might have turned their gifts to Broadway, but now studio techniques had become so essential to pop music that live performance had become a minor consideration in its composition. This music was written to be heard on sound systems, Walkman portables, and compact discs. The synthesizer had become its basic instrument and if this music was ever performed on stage, it was either in videos or in concerts that, as much as possible, were simulations of those videos.

As the 1980s began, however, a younger generation of songwriters had already arisen, led by Marvin Hamlisch (*A Chorus Line*) and Stephen Schwartz (*Godspell, Pippin, The Magic Show*). Hamlisch was a child of the stage, having come up through Broadway's informal apprenticeship system, playing rehearsal piano for Jule Styne's *Funny Girl*. His score for *A Chorus Line*, while informed by musicianly technique and of vast theatrical ambition, was still characterized by the traditional sound of Broadway. However, Hamlisch had a taste for the pop music charts, and in 1979, it was still possible to hope for crossover success. Had he not enjoyed that with "What I Did for Love" from *A Chorus Line*? He decided to go all out for hits with his next show.

They're Playing Our Song is about a couple of lover-songwriters—a likely enough idea for a musical. It was inspired by Hamlisch's romance at the time with lyric writer Carol Bayer Sager, who was to be his collaborator on this show. The book

As a musical about beauty pageants, *Smile* offered promise of a good idea but delivered itself badly.

Above:
The songs for *Baby* were written by Richard Maltby, Jr. and David Shire and presented in the Broadway style at its most sleek and sophisticated. The question was whether there was still an audience for shows with such a style.

Above, right:
A scene from *Falsettoland*.

Right:
Smile proved to be Marvin Hamlisch's first flop.

Left:
Romance, Romance was an intimate Broadway musical in two acts, one of them set most stylishly in the past, as seen here. Intimacy remained one of the most elusive of qualities in big-time musical theater.

Debbie Allen starred in the revival of *Sweet Charity*

was to be written by no less than Neil Simon, who had met Hamlisch while helping out on *A Chorus Line* (he wrote the wisecracks for the tough-talking Sheila). Simon admittedly creates his musicals without worrying about where the songs will fit or what they will be like. It is an old-fashioned approach but, given his comic brilliance, it works for him and certainly did for shows like *Little Me, Sweet Charity*, and *Promises, Promises.* But given Simon's indifference to songs and song spotting, Hamlisch had the freedom to aim for the pop charts with songs tailored to the disco craze.

They're Playing Our Song, however, proved to be a much bigger hit than any of the Hamlisch-Sager songs. For few fashions are as fleeting as those in popular music, and by the time the show opened, disco was virtually passé, making for a poetic justice. Musical theater demands and deserves its own kind of song and a musical style designed for the stage. Marvin Hamlisch has a tremendous gift for this, as he demonstrated with *A Chorus Line*. But *They're Playing Our Song* was a success because of Neil Simon's wonderful humor, not its musicality. This was a comedy with songs and such shows were going to become familiar during the 1980s, musicals that were hits because of the scripts rather than the score. Another example, besides *City of Angels*, is *The Mystery of Edwin Drood*.

Like many composers, Marvin Hamlisch needs a strong director to keep him working toward a purpose greater than a set of good show tunes. But like many successful composers, he has not sought out strong directors, preferring to play the dominant role himself. In a collaborative art, each contributor privately believes that he should be the leader. Some composers are musical dramatists and have the stage sense to conceive works of theater. Andrew Lloyd Webber, for example, has a wonderful stage imagination and Stephen Sondheim is certainly a man of the theater. But such composers are rare, they develop over the course of many shows and even they are better off with directors of equal reputation (or, in Broadway jargon, "clout").

Hamlisch's *Smile* in 1982 started out with a good idea, a satire of American beauty contests adapted from a praised movie of the same name. When Carolyn Leigh, the original lyricist, died in 1983, he teamed up with Howard Ashman, the talented lyricist and director of *The Little Shop of Horrors.* Ashman, however, was the new kid on the block while Hamlisch was a comparative veteran. Under his domination, *Smile* emerged at cross purposes with itself. Like *They're Playing Our Song*, its musical numbers did not seem particularly aware of the rest of the show, and the result was a forty-eight-performance flop.

The next year, perhaps in emulation of Andrew Lloyd Webber, Hamlisch agreed to write a score of virtually continuous music and originate the show in London. The idea had been conceived by a young American lyricist, Christopher Adler (son of Richard Adler, the co-composer of *The Pajama Game* and *Damn Yankees*). It was to be a musical about Jean Seberg, the Midwest actress catapulted out of obscurity by movie producer Otto Preminger, when he cast her as Joan of Arc. She went on to marry the novelist-diplomat Romain Gary, but, upset by scandalous headlines in the tabloid press, she aborted a pregnancy and died soon afterward.

Young Adler saw the stuff of tragic theater in this story and convinced Julian Barry (the author of the play *Lenny*) to write a libretto. Hamlisch wrote the score in the Broadway vernacular but much more ambitiously, in that so much of the dialogue was sung; no less than Sir Peter Hall agreed to produce and direct *Jean* at the prestigious National Theatre of Great Britain, of which he was artistic director.

It was not given a warm welcome. The London press resented this estimable institution being used for the tryout of a commercial American musical even more than it had resented the British *Les Misérables* being tested at the Royal Shakespeare Company. Joining the National Theatre's repertory in the winter of 1983, *Jean* played its seventy-five alloted performances and was never heard from again. It was Hamlisch's last show for the decade.

Of this young generation of composers, Stephen Schwartz's commercial promise seemed the greatest. He was committed to the theater and although his scores for *Godspell, The Magic Show,* and *Pippin* were not distinguished, his stage sense was unmistakable.

The Baker's Wife was Schwartz's first traditional Broadway musical. Both *Godspell* and *Pippin* had originated at theater school (Carnegie Tech) and bore the stigmata of youthful idealism. *The Baker's Wife,* on the other hand, was strictly Broadway. The producer was David Merrick, the librettist Joseph Stein, author of *Fiddler on the Roof.* For the first time, Schwartz wrote conventional, Broadway-type numbers and came up with his most melodious and engaging score to date, but trying out in Los Angeles has become a graveyard tradition. Countless musicals with hit potential have been fixed to death in California—Jerry Herman's *Mack and Mabel,* for instance, Kander and Ebb's *The Act.* An even worse fate befell *The Baker's Wife.* It never even got to Broadway.

Wounded by the setback, Stephen Schwartz has since been battle-shy. He conceived *Working,* a musical version of Studs Terkel's book, but preferred to direct it while sharing composing responsibilities with various pop songwriters. He collaborated with Leonard Bernstein on *Mass,* but wrote only the lyrics. He has not composed an entire show since *The Baker's Wife.*

The likeliest of the new crop of composers and the most *Broadway* of them is a team of great reputation in the theater community but almost unknown to the general public, Richard Maltby, Jr., and David Shire. Without a doubt, they would have joined the working professionals of former generations had Broadway remained Broadway, and surely they were counting on its remaining that when they wrote musicals at Yale on the way to arriving off-Broadway with *The Sap of Life* in 1961.

Shire is a trained musician with a sophisticated stage sense and a gift of melody strong enough to get him popular hits. Maltby is a prodigious lyricist, a brilliant technician with a sophisticated sense of humor that does not preclude tenderness. The songs the team began writing were classic show tunes, truly theatrical in their rhythmic feel, musical turns, and lyric wit. In the 1970s, Maltby and Shire were everyone's discovery after Stephen Sondheim and everyone's choice to be equally famous.

Their chance came with a period (Victorian England) musical called *Love Match* that was produced in 1968 first and, yes, last, in Los Angeles. Shire then found himself writing dance music for Sondheim's *Company* and decided he'd rather go west and write for the movies. Maltby stayed back and learned how to direct by staging plays of Eugene O'Neill and Tennessee Williams. In fact the first Broadway

The Tap Dance Kid was directed by Jerry Zaks, one of the most gifted directors to arrive during the 1980s. Following this debut, he would stage such stylish and refreshing musicals as the hugely successful revival of *Anything Goes* and Stephen Sondheim's *Assassins.*

Overleaf:
This setting for *The Tap Dance Kid* was not as blindingly busy as it seems in this photograph, but neither was it an example of unobtrusive design. A show should not let sets, costumes, or any other production effect dominate. Like the best directing, such elements are most successful when least noticed.

Liz Callaway and Todd Graff, two of Broadway's young and gifted, played the most youthful of the three couples with baby problems in Maltby and Shire's *Baby*.

hit that he would have was going to be not as a lyricist but as the director of the Tony Award–winning revue *Ain't Misbehavin'*.

So it was after twenty years of experience that Maltby and Shire arrived as "overnight" Broadway discoveries with the 1983 musical *Baby*. A sleek and disarming show, it was strongly influenced by Sondheim's *Company* in the non linear, circular form of its libretto and in the contemporary sound of its songs.

Baby is about having babies — or not having them. It is about problems with conception and unexpected pregnancies. Not only is this an unmusical, instructive sort of subject but one suspects that it appealed to the revue mentality in Maltby and Shire. For a book musical, unlike a revue, cannot be tongue-in-cheek for its full length. A story that is not being seriously told cannot provide the basic elements of drama, which are character development, plot conflict, and resolution. But satire works best on the revue floor, in short skits, which is what prompted George S. Kaufman to say that on Broadway, "satire is what closes on Saturday night."

Maltby and Shire, not wanting *Baby* to be a childbirth manual, took a clever approach to their subject, but ended up writing revue material:

Picture a flailin' spermatozoan
Not even knowin' where he is goin'
What's that ahead, a diaphragm? Screw it!
He knows he's dead
My God! He slips through it

This is a smooth lyric, an ingenious one, but it isn't how people talk. It is how clever performers sing in revues. *Baby* was not the best idea for a show, but nevertheless it was one of the most professional and most *Broadway* productions of the decade. Maltby and Shire, who should have been in the process of becoming a major show-writing team, were falling victim to a Broadway that was changing, and strangely enough, Maltby himself would become involved in one of the major shows reflecting those changes when he collaborated on the lyrics for *Miss Saigon*.

If *Baby* was an example of a poor musical theater idea executed with great craftsmanship and even brilliance, *The Tap Dance Kid* (1984) was the reverse — a solidly musical idea poorly executed, albeit by another gifted new composer, Henry Krieger, as well as a new director, Jerry Zaks.

The Tap Dance Kid is the story of a black youngster who has a gift for tap dancing, only to be denied the chance to exploit it by middle-class parents who wish to disassociate themselves from ethnic stereotyping. In urging the young man to study law instead of tap dancing, they deny his gifts and vitality as well as their own heritage.

It was a good idea for a musical as the subject itself is musical as well as rich in symbolism. The point need never have been argued; it was there in the material. Director Zaks, a few years later, would be the toast of New York (directing a revival of *Anything Goes*, as well as the plays *Lend Me a Tenor* and *Six Degrees of Separation*). But he was unable to make a coherent or even professional musical of *The Tap Dance Kid*. As for Henry Krieger, he needed a more experienced, indeed dominating director, as he'd had in Michael Bennett when writing his more ambitious score for *Dreamgirls*. He nevertheless remains one of the bright new composers on Broadway.

Gifted as well is the composer-lyricist Maury Yeston, who had the good fortune to be taken in by the brilliant choreographer-director Tommy Tune for his first two shows. Yeston's *Nine* was an arty project for the generally anti-intellectual Broadway, based as it was on a Federico Fellini film (*8½*). Tune made it into a Tony Award-winning hit (see Chapter 5) but the success was due in greater part to a brilliance of staging rather than to its music. Oddly enough, Yeston wrote more ingratiating and theatrical songs when he was called in to help out with *Grand Hotel*. That music of his was muscular, musicianly, and rich in melody and theatricality.

Perhaps the best kept secret among the newer American composers is Craig Carnelia who, like Yeston, writes his own lyrics. This is always a desirable combination because a composer-lyricist can bring the same sensibility to the words as to his music in a way that teams can only approximate. The lyrics of Irving Berlin, for instance, or Cole Porter, Frank Loesser, or Stephen Sondheim, match their music in mood, in state of mind, in the intricacy or simplicity of the songs. Such music and lyrics are written at the same time, making the melody articulate. A lyricist-composer is especially sensitive to his own cadences and musical stresses, to the emotional nuances of harmonies. He can build to and emphasize his own musical points as Cole Porter did, for instance, in his wonderful "Anything Goes":

> The world has gone mad today
> And good's bad today
> And black's white today
> And day's night today
> When most guys today
> Who women prize today
> Are just silly gigolos

The one-man composer-lyricist is also likelier to respect the rules of prosody because he is so sensitive to his own musical accents. Prosody is the discipline of word meter, and in matters of song, it is used to correct the pronunciation and accentuation of words when they are set to a musical meter. The rules of prosody require that every word be properly pronounced when set to the music, with even the most ingenious rhyme rejected if the words must be stretched, twisted, or in any way mispronounced to fit the music. When Stephen Sondheim describes his wonderfully direct and precise lyrics for *Gypsy* as "neat," it is this correctness of prosody that he means. It is the reason why lyricists are so often word puzzlers. For they have only so many beats in a song and must strike them, precisely, with the same number of syllables while adding their words up to make rhyme and sense.

As a composer-lyricist, Craig Carnelia accepts this challenge to reap its reward. In his only Broadway musical, the most unfortunately titled *Is There Life After High School?*, his songs are characterized by light rock-and-roll rhythms and considerable use of counter melodies. These musical elements are introduced at the outset in Carnelia's sung overture.

> I can see the kid I used to be
> I can feel him tugging at me

As other characters enter the counterpoint, the composer gives them lyrical dialogue.

Above and below: Is There Life After High School? reflected the uniquely sensitive style of composer-lyricist Craig Carnelia.

Although few along Broadway knew it, the late director Michael Bennett had a great deal to do with the discovery of composer–lyricist Rupert Holmes. Based on Bennett's recommendation, Joseph Papp produced Holmes's musical version of Charles Dickens's unfinished *Mystery of Edwin Drood* at the Public Theater. The show was then transferred to Broadway, where it was retitled *Drood* and won a Tony Award. Holmes wrote not only the music and lyrics but the book as well, becoming the first triple-threat man since Meredith Willson and *The Music Man*.

There's a kid inside
And I have him with me always
There's a kid inside
Walking down old high school hallways
There's a kid inside

There's a kid inside

Character A   At a desk
        B   At a dance
        C   In the halls
        D   In the showers

To this very day

Carnelia's sweet sensitivity to the frail and vulnerable egos of teen-agers, their bright confusion and cocky insecurities, is reflected in his edgy yet melodic music. His score for *Is There Life After High School?* is rich and diverse in these respects. But the show was an early (1982) attempt at coping with soaring production costs by mounting small-scaled musicals, and that variance from traditional size, plus the show's rock rhythms, evidently did not appeal to critics or audiences. Overlooked in the process was this extremely impressive debut by an especially gifted and theatrical composer.

Carnelia's abilities were not ignored by the more musically knowledgeable. Stephen Schwartz asked him to contribute to *Working*. Harold Prince engaged him to write songs for an off-Broadway revue. But the human element in Craig Carnelia's

music—his eagerness to write about people and their feelings—was not heavily in demand during a period when Broadway musicals were tending to be about scenic effects.

Besides *Is There Life After High School?* one of the more regrettable victims of this taste for large productions on Broadway was the charming pair of one-act musicals *Romance, Romance.* (Even when produced on the big scale, sets of one-act musicals, *The Apple Tree*, for instance, have not been popular on Broadway.) The first half was a period piece, while the second was set in modern times. Composer Keith Herrmann wrote his songs in corresponding styles. His knowing use of synthesizers gave the music a full and rich sound without a big orchestra in the pit. The small company of actors was attractive, Barry Harmon's direction was stylish, book and lyrics (which he had written himself) were literate, the songs were enchanting, and

The Little Shop of Horrors is a flower shop where a monstrous and carnivorous plant develops — a plant with a hilariously deep, growling, Southern black voice.

173

Ben Harney as the manager of the Dreamgirls singing group gives one of the girls (Loretta Devine) some tough advice.

Opposite:
Henry Krieger's music for *Dreamgirls* ranged from recitative to soul music written in the style of The Supremes, whose career, in fact, inspired the show.

even the reviews were good. Yet with all of that in its favor and a Tony Award nomination as well, *Romance, Romance* barely eked out a season's run in 1988.

If there is any future for smaller-scaled musicals, then, it is cloudy. The only successful one of the entire decade was Alan Mencken's clever and delicious *The Little Shop of Horrors*, whose producers — although Broadway theater owners themselves — wisely kept the show in an off-Broadway house. It is unlikely that it would have been so enduring a success had it been moved to a big theater (witness the 1990 musical *Once on This Island*, which faltered on Broadway after opening most successfully off-Broadway).

Mencken was yet another gifted composer who, in earlier times would have been destined for great things on Broadway. His music for *The Little Shop of Horrors* was in deft parody of the *doo-wop* popular music of the 1960s, but the producing stakes on Broadway had discouraged relaxed creativity. Mencken went, instead, to Hollywood where he wrote the acclaimed score for the movie *The Little Mermaid*.

Yet another praised newcomer to get a first hearing off-Broadway, and perhaps the most highly praised of all, was William Finn. His three "Marvin" one-act musicals, *In Trousers*, *The March of the Falsettos*, and *Falsettoland*, were each greeted with approval and prizes. They were clever and touching, which is a rare combination. Like the big British musicals, Finn's were entirely sung but his music was in the Broadway style. It was also melodically weak. The greater talent seemed to lie in his words, which managed to combine the purposes of dialogue and lyrics, making sung conversation sound natural and clear.

Finn's work was regularly smart and often brilliant but small in scale and in effect. Broadway, again, is a theater of size. His talent is unmistakable but his future remains uncertain.

Indeed, all this promise from all these composers remains in the form that the future always takes in the theater — talented people. This is a sizable and impressive group of composers and lyricists — Hamlisch, Schwartz, Maltby and Shire, and the rest. Moreover, Broadway has also gained the vastly gifted Andrew Lloyd Webber, whose series of immense successes will forever characterize the 1980s, as well as the team of Claude-Michel Schönberg and Alain Boublil, authors of *Les Misérables* and *Miss Saigon*.

It would be foolishly jingoistic as well as illogical to insist on Broadway musicals being written only by Americans. Whether a musical is created and first produced in New York, London, or Paris does not determine its genre or right to belong. The love for Broadway musicals, like any love, is all-trusting and grateful.

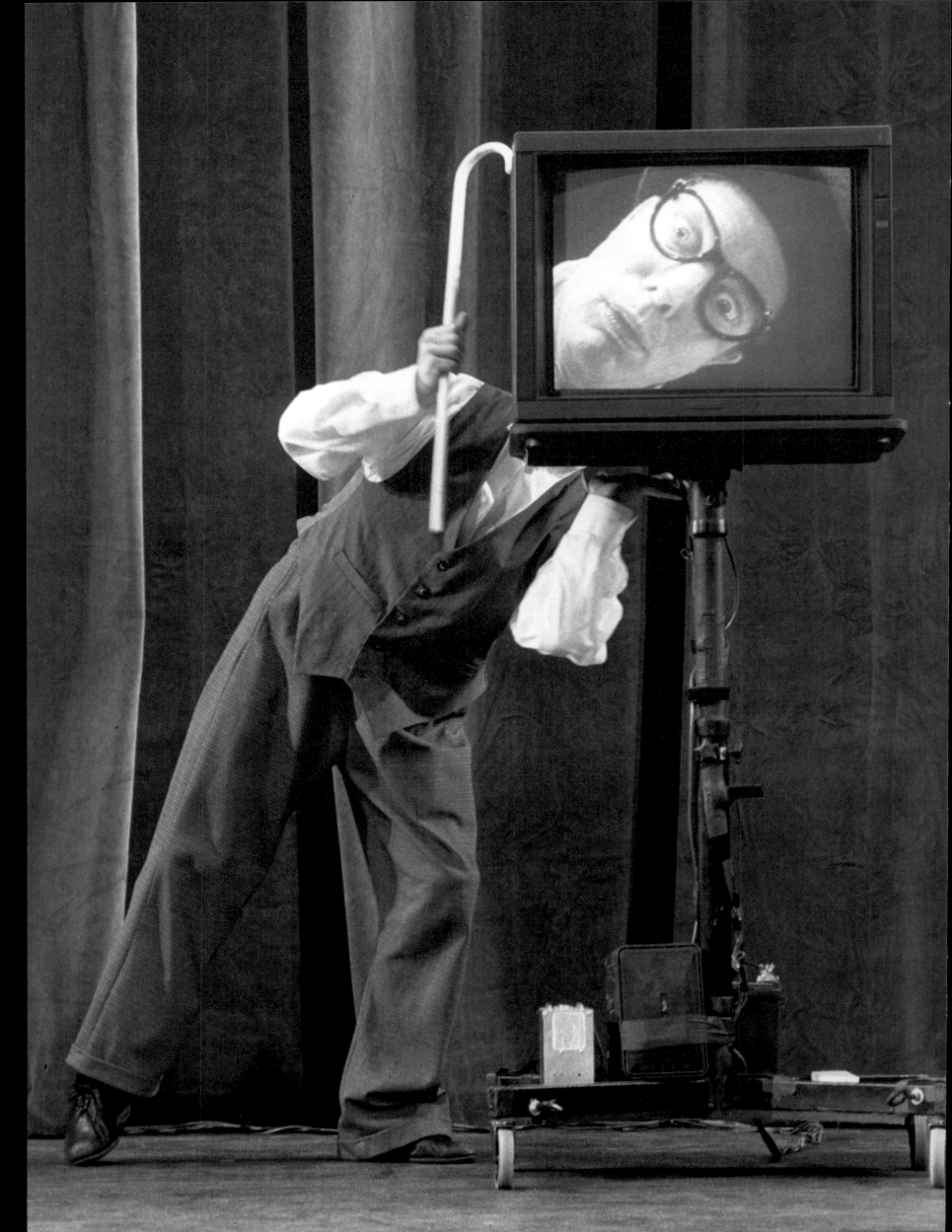

CHAPTER
10
DIFFERENT

Not every musical on Broadway is a *Broadway musical*. Occasionally, something that does not fit the standard mold slips through—a different kind of show, for the possibilities of musical theater are not apparent only to song and dance people. Long before the tap dancing and tootsies of our musical comedies, the ancient Greeks, for instance, had created incantational rituals that made for a somewhat different kind of theater. In later eras, the British had their masques and the Japanese their kabuki. Today, in the various studios of the world's greater downtown there are constant theater experiments, and probably the most flourishing of developments in the contemporary New York avant-garde has been performance art, a cross between living tableau, cabaret, and modern dance.

On Broadway, such alternative forms of musical theater do not slip through the traditional mesh very often. Progress in Broadway musicals, as in general, is the effect of the actions of impatient radicals upon stubborn traditionalists. Broadway is a conventional world and conventional musicals are its top attraction. There, progress is slow because of its resistance to change. When something different does appear in the thick of the chorus lines, the experiment usually blows up in its inventor's face because a commercial theater is an unlikely and inhospitable laboratory. The "different" musical, then, whether arty, or naive, or original and wonderful, can anticipate disdain on Broadway, and not just from show people but even perhaps from the very drama critics who are supposed to be open-minded. Too often reviewers serve as protectors of the establishment.

Because the techniques of professional theater—lighting, set design, costumes, orchestration—have been mastered by those with the most experience, sleek production values tend to be found only in the standard product and these values are frequently taken, or mistaken, for professionalism. Sometimes, though, a different kind of musical will be professionally crafted and on rare occasions will even prove interesting or, heaven help Broadway, enjoyable. Many of these shows do not have songs or singing. Most have no speaking but, rather, a great deal of music with

However the technology of it worked, getting Bill Irwin's face onto the television monitor made for a disarming and hilarious moment in Largely New York. It transcended differences between commercial entertainment and avant-garde performance art.

With exquisite tension, Bunny Briggs in *Black and Blue* dances to Duke Ellington's rhapsodic and utterly beatless "In a Sentimental Mood."

movement set to it, musical staging perhaps, rather than dance as such. Examples have been as diverse as the ritualistic spectacles of Max Reinhardt in the thirties or, more recently, the sculpted figures of the Swiss dance-mime troupe Mummenchanz.

Mummenchanz enjoyed quite a success in New York toward the end of the 1970s, bewildering Broadway but not its audiences. The little show ran no fewer than 1,326 performances before closing in 1980, and then came back a couple of seasons later to resume its run with a second edition. Perhaps its triumph was in part due to its appeal to youngsters and the greater ability of children to adapt to novelty and abstraction. For adults, generally speaking, the unusual musical is rarely successful; and if by chance one does find an audience, the collectively knowledgeable Broadway heads are promptly buried in the sand. They do not want to know how such a thing (as *Hair*, for instance) could happen.

In 1977, a show called *Beatlemania* moved into New York's venerable Winter Garden Theatre where it played to sell-out business for *two years* without its existence being acknowledged by the news media. As far as the press was concerned, the production just was not there, and this was unfortunate because whatever its shortcomings, *Beatlemania* was a fascinating exercise in theater as reality.

It was a replica of a Beatles concert, one that was taken for the thing itself. This was a memorable example of an audience willingly "suspending disbelief" (as the theater experience is frequently defined). The youthful spectators knew that they were not seeing the real Beatles in a real concert; indeed, at that time the Beatles no longer existed. But the audience was so eager to experience a Beatles concert that for the duration of the show, they accepted four impersonators singing and playing the Beatles repertoire done in the classic arrangements as if they were in fact the Beatles. Moreover, the audience entered into the delusion, behaving as if they were at such a concert, screaming, dancing, even smoking in the theater. The show had been designed to inspire and support this self-deception, and in that design it succeeded absolutely. Yet, fascinating as the phenomenon was, it was not deemed worthy of notice or review because *Beatlemania* did not fit into preexisting classifications. It wasn't a rock concert and it certainly wasn't a Broadway musical.

Broadway is understandably proud of its musicals. They are unique and special. But the only musicals it recognizes are those made in the original mold, the song-and-dance shows that begin with overtures, end with walk-out music, and sandwich assorted production numbers, comedy turns, ballads, and showstoppers in-between. That is the basic reason why Andrew Lloyd Webber's musicals have been met with such resistance from the show-business establishment. They are not the old song and dance.

Beloved as that tradition may be, it is not so delicate as to need protection from alternate approaches. There are, after all, other kinds of theater, and if Broadway's musicals don't learn from them and grow, they will atrophy and die. But few producers are willing to risk Broadway-sized investments on behalf of untraditional musicals that audiences *might* like. Too, most producers have conservative taste.

One who doesn't, and who produced three unconventional musicals during the 1980s, is Jules Fisher, a lighting designer whose career developed along perfectly traditional lines. Too ambitious to limit himself to lighting and too imaginative to hold his horizons at the line of musical comedy, he became involved with the designing of light shows for rock concerts. This was the beloved music of his youth, and he was convinced that some of the techniques developed in those concerts, particulary in regard to slide and film projections, could be used to advantage in the theater. He investigated the use of mixed media — live action and film — in theater as he projected slides and movie clips onto backdrops or scrims of varying sizes.

His first application of this technique was for a simple touring production of the first "rock opera" *Tommy* by The Who. The lessons he learned were applied to *Beatlemania* as he tried to set this simulated concert in the context of its times.

Refining the techniques for synchronizing film and slide projections with live action, Fisher produced a more elaborate musical in 1983, one again based on the popular music he loved so well. This was *Rock 'n' Roll! The First Five Thousand Years* an imaginative and exciting presentation of America's early rock-and-roll acts, performers who were stylishly impersonated and worked theatrically into a show that was neither a book musical nor a revue but a thing of its own kind. Fisher put this production into a major Broadway theater, but that did not convince theatergoers that it was a legitimate show. Being reviewed by pop music critics rather than theater critics, even being favorably reviewed, hardly sold tickets to theatergoers either. *Rock 'n' Roll! The First Five Thousand Years* was one of the most entertaining, and certainly one of the most original, musicals to be presented on Broadway during the 1980s but it was also one of the most unappreciated. It closed after nine performances.

Fisher remained convinced that his idea was technically and aesthetically sound. In 1989 he produced and designed *Elvis — A Musical Celebration*, and to strengthen its theatrical aspects, he engaged a major Broadway choreographer-director, Patricia Birch, to stage it. Collaborating with her, his technological ingenuity now dovetailed with his artistic purposes. Film and live performance were synchronized and blended as never before. Perhaps there were times during *Elvis* when the technical achievements were so ingenious that the production seemed to be showing them off, but that is inevitable in the first blush of a new technique. For the most part, *Elvis* was an exciting kind of musical. Some of its purely theatrical notions were immensely dramatic, such as having three different actors play Presley at different ages, sometimes on stage simultaneously. The charisma of Presley the entertainer lashed painfully against the tragedy of Presley as a victim of his own success.

This time, Fisher first sent his show on a cross-country tour. Audiences away from New York are not nearly so rigid as Broadway's. Inevitably, but warily, bringing it to New York, he chose a theater that was devoted to rock concerts, hoping to attract younger, music-oriented audiences. But the problem remained — the audience was not getting what it expected. This was not a rock concert any more than it was a Broadway musical, and audiences wanted to know what they were getting *before* they paid for it. So, *Elvis* failed in New York.

Jules Fisher remained certain that his technological developments could make an exciting kind of musical, and he wanted desperately to unite his beloved rock-and-roll music with the theater, but as a producer, he understood all too well the inflexible reality of the bottom line.

The legendary Ruth Brown appeared in *Black and Blue*.

Overleaf:
The style of *Black and Blue* was refreshing on a Broadway that had been accustomed to traditional glitter. It had a period chic that was purely European. Being entirely sung and without dialogue, it also had great appeal for foreign tourists.

A more successful deviation from standard Broadway fare was *Tango Argentino*, imported from South America and first presented in New York City's huge City Center Theater for a limited engagement. It was an evening of tango dancing performed by a small troupe, and yet it was by no means a dance recital. The tango is not only a romantic and sexy dance but also in some ways a ritual of mating, one that involves lure, resistance, domination, danger, conquest, and uncertain victory. This Argentinian company made tango dancing particularly erotic for American audiences, presenting a sexuality very different from what we are accustomed to on our stages and movie screens.

For the dancers in *Tango Argentino* were not the young and attractive performers typical in popular American romance. These men were middle-aged, paunchy and balding. The women were fiery but not picture-perfect beauties; they all seemed to have traveled down a few roads. The sensual electricity was palpable. They would dance and exchange partners, by turns intense or flirtatious, teasing, angry. Limbs would entwine as if already in the act of love. The small onstage band with its accordion and handful of violins seemed provincial, even tacky, especially when playing orchestral selections between dances, but what emanated overall was a feeling of sexuality in a dance hall down some Buenos Aires side street.

The "Beatles," young and old, in *Beatlemania* were played by Mitch Weissman (Paul), Joe Pecorino (John), Leslie Fradkin (George), and Justin McNeil (Ringo). *Beatlemania* so differed from conventional Broadway fare that critics refused to review it, but young audiences kept it running for years.

183

This sense of displacement and transport lies at the heart of theater, and when enthusiastic audiences encouraged the producers to transfer *Tango Argentino* to a regular theater for an extended engagement, the show went to Broadway. Even though it wasn't *Hello, Dolly!*, it was one of the successes of the 1985 season.

In 1989 the same producers brought another unconventional show to Broadway. *Black and Blue* used Afro-American materials—jazz and blues, tap dancing and cakewalks—setting them with a sleek stylishness that lent them a European sensibility, as if they came from the black expatriate world in Paris during the thirties. The music might be Duke Ellington's or down-and-dirty blues from the Deep South, and the dancing might be fancy tap steps by a line of men in top hats and tails or shuffles from old vaudeville, but in the monochromatic shades and symmetric patterns there emerged an Art Deco chic to *Black and Blue* that made it seem deliciously elegant. It was a counter-image to the strange, Lucite, and white world of Astaire and Rogers in their never-never-land movie Venices. From the singing and choreography to the costume and lighting design, this show was a museum-quality vision, and although it was at first overshadowed by *Jerome Robbins' Broadway*, perhaps a Tony Award winner but a depressingly backward-looking show, two years later *Black and Blue* was still running at the Minskoff Theatre while *Jerome Robbins' Broadway* had closed.

Black and Blue was unique, then, and it had a unique vision of itself.

An even more unusual musical on Broadway during the 1980s was Bill Irwin's *Largely New York*, which was as American in sensibility as *Black and Blue* was European. This intermissionless ninety-minute show managed to fashion theater of general appeal out of the language and devices of the avant-garde New York art world. It combined video techniques, modern dance, mime, and performance art, and its full title suggested how unlikely a Broadway candidate it was: *Largely New York—The Further Adventures of a Post-Modern Hoofer.* Yet the title also suggested its ambitiousness, seeking to find a link between vaudeville and avant-garde performance art. The former had roots in traditional entertainment, while the latter could be seen through esoteric eyes.

Either way, Broadway audiences responded to Bill Irwin's stage character, a Chaplinesque Everyman wandering through a bewildering New York downtown art world. Without speaking, singing, or dancing in any formal sense, Irwin was on stage for virtually the entire show. He might be responding to a beautiful dancer who is practicing before a television camera, dealing with her first in the flesh, then as an image on a screen, and finally with his own image on that screen. Or he might be coping with a group of academics in caps and gowns, or aliens from some modern dance company; he might be grappling with the phenomenon of a disobedient curtain, or with two young black men and their boombox rap music. Certainly, Irwin did none of the things that Broadway audiences expect on their musical stage except for one item: he entertained with humanity.

Largely New York was not a smash hit but for such a show to run several months in a big Broadway theater made it as much of a success, in a way, as *The Phantom of the Opera.*

Not only was this show about performance art but it was also an *example* of performance art, a movement that originated in the avant-garde art world of the

1960s and 1970s and then was adopted by artistic adventures in theater, music video, and cabaret. Performance art was originally an exploration by visual artists of time, space, and materials, making "real life" the canvas on which their ideas about movement, form, the artist, and art were "painted." Gradually, younger artists made these "happenings" entertaining, adding elements of humor or storytelling and this form became more theatricalized, leaving the art studios for stages and audiences. Bill Irwin introduced mime, vaudeville, and comedy, the sense of entertainment.

The giant of a more formal avant-garde theater has been Robert Wilson, who used elements of performance art in a series of stunning spectacles. Trained as an architect, Wilson turned to choreography and rose to prominence in the 1970s under the sponsorship of no less than Jerome Robbins when the great choreographer was privately exploring artistic possibilities of musical theater in a richly subsidized workshop he called the American Laboratory Theater. From the outset, Robert Wilson's theater work was based on architectural imagery. The stage pictures he created were so physical, so elaborate—they were so beautifully and accessibly surreal and employed such large companies of performers—that it was difficult to understand how he managed to finance these productions for engagements of only three or four performances.

Presented in enormous theaters like the Brooklyn Academy of Music or even the Metropolitan Opera House, they had almost continuous music, with choreographed movement that floated at a trancelike pace, as if frozen in time. They bore strange titles like *The Life and Times of Josef Stalin* or *Einstein on the Beach*. A single production might last twelve or fourteen hours, its mood dreamy and its language incoherent (in fact Wilson used texts that were written by an autistic adolescent to break English down to its unprotected basics).

Ordinarily, such avant-garde theater is of interest only to the most esoteric of audiences but Robert Wilson had a genius for broadly appealing magic, pictures, and even fun. In 1974 his *A Letter for Queen Victoria* was actually produced on Broadway. That was somewhat optimistic and doomed to failure, but Wilson had become internationally celebrated and a revival of his *Einstein on the Beach* at the Metropolitan Opera House in New York was one of the major theater events of the 1970s. While general audiences may not be aware of his work, his influence is vast and it is hard to imagine rock music videos, for example, without his pioneering, surreal stage visions. He did what Jerome Robbins, a great artist of course, could not do on Broadway or even in the relatively liberal world of ballet. But if works such as Robert Wilson's, or of the performance artists, are not likely ever to attract mass audiences on Broadway, they still offer visions of the potential in musical theater. We have everything to learn, gain, adopt, and, heaven help us, even enjoy from music theater of a different kind.

Critical enthusiasm and the patronage of New York's artistic and intellectual world did not count for much at the box office when director–creator Robert Wilson offered his avant-garde musical theater on Broadway with *A Letter for Queen Victoria*.

190

On a male-dominated Broadway, *The Secret Garden* was written by women (book and lyrics by Marsha Norman, music by Lucy Simon) and it was directed by a woman, Susan B. Schulman. The resulting musical was not only artistically different but different in sensibility from traditionally "tough" shows.

CHAPTER

11

WALK
OUT
MUSIC

If the beloved, traditional Broadway show was based on a model slowly growing outmoded — and dependent on past generations of showmakers — no further proof of its looming obsolescence was necessary than the death notices of the 1980s. One could not only see theater history passing through those obituaries but also Broadway's need for revitalization — for fresh ideas and new blood. For it was painfully plain that, from the 101-year-old Irving Berlin to the 44-year-old Michael Bennett, those who had been producing, writing, directing, and starring in all the wonderful Broadway shows were people of past and disappearing generations. The roll call was all the more grievous for its shock of talent. Broadway musicals had developed so many gifted creators. Who was to replace them?

Irving Berlin and Richard Rodgers lead the memorial list of course, the last remaining Giants among our stage composers. It was Rodgers who died first (1979), working until the end. He had never really survived the 1960 death of Oscar Hammerstein II. He subsequently wrote his own lyrics for *No Strings* and collaborated with Stephen Sondheim (*Do I Hear a Waltz?*), Martin Charnin (*Two by Two*), and Sheldon Harnick (*Rex*), but he could never regain the popular touch that had borne him through two great partnerships, the first, of course, having been with Lorenz Hart. His style had changed in a startling way when, in 1943, he abandoned Hart to team with Hammerstein and write *Oklahoma!* The Dick Rodgers who had composed so many lilting melodies with Larry Hart became a Richard Rodgers of sober theater music. While he never lost his genius for melody, in working with the theatrically ambitious Hammerstein he turned more attention to suiting music to drama, character, and dialogue. As a result, while Rodgers had written his best songs with Hart, he would write his best theater music with Hammerstein, and, as if realizing that, he attempted similar musical plays after his partner's death.

Above, and opposite: Richard Rodgers's last show was I Remember Mama, *starring Liv Ullmann.*

I Remember Mama was such a show, a musicalization of a John Van Druten play that Rodgers and Hammerstein had produced themselves in 1944. Some years later it became well known as the basis of a TV show, but the series ran in the earliest days of television and not many 1979 theatergoers could have remembered it.

The musical was troubled from the outset. There were hints of the formidable Rodgers gifts in some of its songs, but it was lurchingly dramatic and old-fashioned. If proof was necessary that times had changed, well there it was. The musical play that Oscar Hammerstein II had worked so long at developing now seemed to be just that, a *musical play*, while the musical theater had meanwhile developed a character all its own, divorced from conventional drama and allied, instead, with choreography and a more nonlinear style of storytelling. Of course, there would always be room for any show that, as they say on Broadway, *works*, but it was increasingly apparent that few traditional, or "book," musicals would ever work again. The dispirited production ran a humiliating 108 performances and became the first Richard Rodgers show in a half century to go without a recording. The composer died at the end of 1979, four months after it closed. (Some years later the original cast was reassembled and an album was made.)

Five years after Richard Rodgers's death, there was a third Broadway revival of *The King and I*, his best and most popular show. As had become customary, the star was the original King, Yul Brynner. The actor, who was both rewarded and saddled with the role of a lifetime, seemed able to make a hit out of any version of *The King and I*, but nothing else. He became a prisoner of it, very much like Eugene O'Neill's father James with his *Count of Monte Cristo*. The last Brynner *King and I* closed on Broadway because of the star's own, fatal illness, an irony considering the physical vitality that he brought to the role. His final performance in 1985 was, quite amazingly, his 4,631st!

Irving Berlin's death in 1989 was even more of a national event than Rodgers's because of his age, because of the unique identification he had with American consciousness, and because, having been a semirecluse for so many years, he had become a kind of mythic figure.

Of the five musical Giants, Berlin was best known to the public because he wrote so many freestanding, nontheatrical or popular songs, and such songs are generally better known than showtunes. More to the point, several of them had become part of the country's heritage, such as "White Christmas" and "Easter Parade," while "God Bless America" was virtually a second national anthem. Other tunes were simply beloved: "Always," for instance, "How Deep Is the Ocean?" or "Blue Skies." And Berlin had also come to be identified with a patriotic sensibility by writing and appearing in the wartime shows *Yip, Yip, Yaphank* and *This Is the Army*.

His Broadway presence was less noticeable. Until *Annie Get Your Gun* in 1946, he had never written a successful "book" musical, only revues, those plotless shows comprised of comedy sketches and musical numbers, such as his *As Thousands Cheer* and the various *Music Box Revues* (named for the Music Box Theatre, which he co-owned with the Shubert Organization). Book musicals are remembered and revived, the shows whose songs are instantly identified with them. We think not of the "Soliloquy," but the "'Soliloquy' from *Carousel*," "'Shall We Dance' from *The King and*

IRVING BERLIN

Reclusive as Irving Berlin was, he loved to talk shop on the telephone. "My best song?" he once mused. "No, 'Always' isn't my best song, and not 'Blue Skies' either, or 'Easter Parade,' and as for 'Remember,' well that's just a tune. My best song is 'God Bless America' and I'll tell you why 'God Bless America' is my best song, because it sold more records and sheet music, it made more money than any other of my stuff, including 'White Christmas.' That's why 'God Bless America' is my best song."

Berlin wasn't being materialistic. He had endowed colleges with the royalties from some of his most enduring songs. He was simply speaking as a professional songwriter and was saying that popular music was not worthy of pretentious discussions about better and best. The only measure that mattered was the commercial measure of sales.

As for the writing of lyrics, he was similarly down-to-earth. "The way to do it is very simple," he said on the telephone. "Suppose you're writing 'There's No Business Like Show Business.' What you do is, when you come up with a punch line, let's say it's about becoming a star overnight, you work backwards from it so you can set it up. Then you can hit them with a bang with, 'Next day on your dressing room they've hung a star.'

"It's that simple," he said.

Just as simple, he said, was the mystery of writing so many songs that came to be identified with Fred Astaire. Songs like "Let's Face the Music and Dance," "Cheek to Cheek," "It Only Happens when I Dance with You," and "Let Yourself Go." Berlin laughed and said, "It's no mystery, writing for Astaire. He's a dancer. I write songs for him about dancing.

"See?" Irving Berlin said. "Easy."

Irving Berlin.

Alan Jay Lerner and Frederick Loewe bequeathed several classics to lovers of Broadway musicals. *Brigadoon* will surely be reproduced through the years. This revival featured ice skater John Curry as the doomed Scottish dancer, Harry.

I," "'The Rain in Spain' from *My Fair Lady,*" "'Memory' from *Cats,*" and so on. Berlin's "Easter Parade" may be beloved but we do not think of it as "'Easter Parade' from *As Thousands Cheer.*"

It was not until he wrote a book musical *(Annie Get Your Gun)* that Berlin was established as a Broadway composer, and he would write only one more book musical hit, *Call Me Madam.* His final work, *Mr. President* in 1962, was a cheerfully blatant attempt to capitalize on his patriotic reputation, but although the show had an immense advance sale, it was unenthusiastically received and ran only briefly. The composer was then seventy-four and the only new song that would be heard from him after that was "An Old-Fashioned Wedding," written for a revival of *Annie Get Your Gun* at Lincoln Center.

When Berlin died in September, 1989, the country mourned as it hadn't for any other composer. His death signified the end of a national fantasy — that there was a virtuous America beyond reproach, an America that had fought for democracy and won, an America that flew its banner of equality and liberty without hesitation or doubt. Berlin's vision was of a nation as white as its Christmases and as Christian as well, and, in the bargain, well dressed for Easter Parades. Perhaps that America had never existed, but now even the fantasy was gone, destroyed during the Vietnam years and interred with Irving Berlin. It was indeed something to mourn, the loss of so idealized an image, however insubstantial. For it was a kind of aspiration.

During the 1980s there were other deaths among the aging generation of Master composers, for instance, Alan Jay Lerner and Frederick Loewe, the creators

of *Brigadoon, My Fair Lady,* and *Camelot.* But the most jolting death in this generation of composers was Leonard Bernstein's in 1990; that was because he seemed eternally young. There was such vitality in Bernstein's music, conducting, and attitude toward work and life, that he came to represent artistic energy itself.

Bernstein wrote only four musicals — why count the seven-performance 1976 disaster *1600 Pennsylvania Avenue?*

From the first jazzy drumbeats of his *On the Town* overture it was clear that someone had arrived with a new voice for Broadway and a musicianly love of the old show tune. This was the first of three Bernstein "New York" shows; the same edgy urbanity would characterize his scores for *Wonderful Town* and the masterpiece *West Side Story.* He could somehow write the most complex music and make it seem theatrical and *show business.* Who else would have delighted in using the same four notes in completely different ways to start two utterly dissimilar songs, "Maria" and "Cool"?

Similarly, only a raving genius would have the knowledge, taste, and training simultaneously to satirize and invent his own version of Jacques Offenbach for the dazzling score of *Candide.* And every scrap of his Broadway writing demonstrates the significance of his musicianship, for not a note of it sounds dated, only young and so terrifically alive. Bernstein's decision to abandon Broadway and concentrate on conducting and composing classical music was understandable, but it created a tremendous loss for a theater that he would surely have remade, as he indeed began to do with *West Side Story.* His death at the age of 73 proved that if someone so vital as Leonard Bernstein could die, then anyone could.

Still another Master who died during the decade was Harold Arlen (in 1986). Arlen's songs are unique and musically ambitious: "Come Rain or Come Shine," for instance, for *St. Louis Woman,* or "A Sleepin' Bee" for *House of Flowers,* and most ambitiously of all, "The Man That Got Away" for the movie *A Star Is Born.* But they are songs for their own sake, and it was Arlen's inability to seek out the larger theatrical purpose, to link songs to the story at hand, as well as his devotion to popular music, that stifled his stage career and even prematurely ended his songwriting. He was so discouraged by the popularity of rock-and-roll that he stopped composing for the theater, as if the ultimate purpose of a musical's score was to launch one or two songs onto what was then called "the hit parade" (later, *the charts*). Nor was Arlen the only talented composer to be frustrated by a misguided interest in hit songs. Frank Loesser and Harry Warren also lost their enthusiasm because of changing taste in American popular music.

No less jolting a reminder of the loss of Broadway greats during the 1980s were the deaths of such musical comedy stars as Rex Harrison, Robert Preston, Ray Bolger, Danny Kaye, and Phil Silvers, and such delightful character actors as George Rose and Jack Gilford.

Then there was Fred Astaire. The elegant and thrilling dancer is now beloved for leading Ginger Rogers through a series of devastatingly sophisticated movie musicals with scores by Kern, Gershwin, Berlin, and Porter, but he had begun as a Broadway star, partnering his sister Adele through *Lady Be Good* and *Funny Face.* Brilliant dancer though he was, Astaire could not have anticipated the dominating roles that choreographers would come to play on Broadway, while dancing stars faded away. In Astaire's era, even when America's greatest choreographer, George Balanchine, staged dances on Broadway for such shows as *The Boys from Syracuse* and *On Your Toes*, "choreography" merely meant dance numbers. In the 1960s and 1970s, dance and musical staging became so important that direction and choreography merged. Perhaps the most devastating deaths of the decade were in precisely this area, the choreographer-directors, for not only did Balanchine himself die (in 1983), but also Gower Champion (1979), Michael Bennett and Bob Fosse (1987), and Ron Field (1988). In short, during this span of time, the vibrant and creative community of choreographic directors was decimated.

None came to a more melodramatic end than Champion, whose death was announced onstage on the opening night of *42nd Street*, the biggest hit of his career. On the other hand, Fosse's last show *Big Deal* was his only Broadway failure. Fosse and Champion are a study in contrasts. They worked together as minor movie actors in 1952 at MGM. Champion was already the better established, having come to Hollywood with his wife, Marge, after they had achieved some success as a nightclub and television dance team. He had already choreographed *Lend an Ear* on Broadway. Fosse had been half a dance team too, Fosse and Niles, but he had broken up the act as well as the marriage to pursue a movie career. He did not pursue it for long. Hollywood musicals were going out of fashion when he was given the startling opportunity to choreograph a Broadway show despite his absolute lack of experience. It was 1954's *Pajama Game* and with one number, "Steam Heat," Fosse established himself as an original. Although several of his later shows (*The Conquering Hero, Pleasures and Palaces*) would close out of town, he never came into New York with anything but a hit until *Big Deal*, his last show, in 1986.

Gower Champion gave the movies more of a try but he, too, returned to Broadway to direct as well as choreograph such hits as *Bye Bye Birdie, Carnival, Hello, Dolly!*, and *I Do, I Do!* Fosse became a director with *Redhead* at about the same time as Champion did with *Birdie*. Although Fosse's hits — *Sweet Charity, Dancin', Chicago* — were never as long-running as Champion's, his reputation was loftier. A cynic, Fosse tended toward dark material, while Champion's shows seem mere entertainments, and cynicism gets more respect. Of course, there is nothing "mere" about any musical. The challenge and difficulty of making a good show are related not to subject matter or thematic purpose but to artistic inspiration and craftsmanship. Nevertheless, the pure entertainment value of *Hello, Dolly!*, for instance, cost Champion credit for the real brilliance of the work in it.

Also, Bob Fosse was the only director of Broadway musicals who also triumphed as a film director. (Herbert Ross never succeeded on Broadway as he did in Hollywood, and Jerome Robbins gave up on directing movies halfway through filming *West Side Story*). Fosse's triumphant 1973, when he won an Academy Award (*Cabaret*), a Tony (*Pippin*), and an Emmy ("*Liza with a 'Z'*"), will probably never be matched.

He probably would never have directed another musical had it not been for the failure of his 1984 movie *Star 80*. He had always believed that his true destiny was in Hollywood. Three of his five movies had been nominated for an Academy Award — *Cabaret, Lenny,* and *All That Jazz*. That was perhaps even more impressive,

At top: Ethel Merman.
Above: Mary Martin.

Overleaf:
The vitality of Bob Fosse's last choreography, this dance in *Big Deal*, came in stark contrast to the blackness that his gloom imposed on the show.

199

Bob Fosse choreographs Sandahl Bergman for *Dancin'*.

if less glittering, than winning all those prizes in one year. But the chronically pessimistic Fosse was convinced that *Star 80* had finished him in Hollywood. It was probably the reason he returned to Broadway in 1986, eleven years after he had done the musical *Chicago*.

Decades earlier he had bought the rights to an Italian movie, *Big Deal on Madonna Street*, with the intention of musicalizing it for the stage. After trying countless approaches (one of them involving a Mexican setting and mariachi music), he now wrote his own script for a setting among blacks in Chicago during the Depression. It was all too apt a setting for the dark-mooded Fosse.

He wrote his own libretto because, like Jerome Robbins, he had been frustrated by the collaborative nature of musical-making, with its inevitable artistic compromises. For this same reason, he used period songs written by dead composers.

As if to make the movie that he believed was being denied him in Hollywood, Fosse tried to make *Big Deal* into a cinematic production. "That's meant to be a dissolve," he would tell his lighting designer, Jules Fisher, "and this is supposed to be a cross-fade." His gloom became literalized as he ordered the set designer, Peter Larkin, to spray all the scenery with black paint "even though," Larkin said, "everyone knows that if a stage is dark or black long enough, the audience loses its concentration." Among Fosse's dance assistants, there were whispers that he had lost interest in choreography.

Big Deal opened to disastrous reviews. Ironically, Fosse had another show on Broadway only a few weeks later, a revival of his 1966 *Sweet Charity*, which he was also directing. So it happened that while *Big Deal* was becoming his first Broadway flop, *Sweet Charity* was a hit, and it seemed to suggest that on a Broadway of *Evita* and *Cats*, a Bob Fosse musical had become nostalgia.

Do people die of disappointment? Can an artist be rejected to death? Bob Fosse died only a year later, collapsing on a Washington, D.C., street corner on the opening night there of *Sweet Charity*.

The star of that touring company was Donna McKechnie, who, only months earlier, had been devastated by the death of her former husband, Michael Bennett. *A Chorus Line* had caused many to call him a genius, but some questioned that and others envied it, and many along bitchy Broadway hoped for his quick comeuppance. Bennett had worked hard to earn a reputation as a top choreographer, having created the dances for *Promises, Promises, Company*, and *Follies. A Chorus Line*, however, was his first show as a director (he had received co-director credit for *Follies*), and some felt that he simply had not done enough work to rank with Jerome Robbins, Bob Fosse, or Gower Champion, who had so many shows behind them.

Too, *A Chorus Line* was a tough act to follow. While Bennett could not concern himself with the envy of others, he did seem to respond to the psychological circumstance, and, as if to avoid comparisons, his next musical was more traditional and less ambitious. *Ballroom*, despite a setting that suggested possibilities for a concept musical, was a conventional show, a book musical. Based on a sentimental television movie about the romance of an unexceptional, middle-class, middle-aged couple on the dance floor of a New York ballroom, it was *Marty* set to a fox trot. With

202

a characterless musical score, and after unusually unpleasant script troubles, *Ballroom* became a show without an indentity. It seemed to lack a conscious stage purpose, as if it existed merely to be the show Bennett did after *A Chorus Line*, the way *Camelot* was the show that Lerner and Loewe did after *My Fair Lady*.

However, Bennett's subsequent musical was indeed a worthy successor to *A Chorus Line*, in no way imitative while taking concept musicals to an even higher plane of development. *Dreamgirls* was inspired by the singing group the Supremes, with a script and lyrics by the off-Broadway playwright Tom Eyen and music by newcomer Henry Krieger (like George Abbott, Michael Bennett preferred to work with inexperienced composers).

Dreamgirls was a backstage musical about greed, ambition, and artistic compromise, symbolized by the corruption of soul music so that it might sell to a white public. For Bennett, a show about musical performers meant that many of its numbers could be "justified," that is, they would be performed only where musical numbers would be performed in real life. Most of the musical numbers in *A Chorus Line* were, in that sense, justified.

But unjustifiably (in that sense), the show relied on extensive *recitative* music — as in opera — the singing of dialogue. Bennett had long been seeking the all-musical musical — thus far, through constant choreography. Now he seemed to be incorporating the technique of Andrew Lloyd Webber's "through-composed" shows, using continuous singing.

The scenery that Robin Wagner designed was minimal but startling: four giant, remote-controlled towers that danced along the stage, gliding and rotating as

203

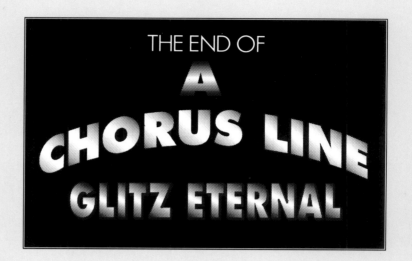

THE END OF
A Chorus Line
GLITZ ETERNAL

Seldom had the inevitable come with such surprise. After fifteen years on Broadway, *A Chorus Line* was scheduled to close on March 31, 1990, with its 6,014th performance. "The End of the Line" was the headline on its last advertisement. Well there are worse disasters, and fifteen years wasn't bad for a Broadway show, but of course *A Chorus Line* was not just a Broadway show. Being about a mythic kind of musical it became a myth itself, and it always seemed to be there at the Shubert Theater on West 44th Street, across the street from Sardi's restaurant, the historic theatrical gathering place, where it was supposed to be. Other shows might come and go, but ever since 1975 and all through the 1980s, *A Chorus Line* remained, complete with the old blurbs from the old critics in the old newspapers, etched in the great mirrors outside the theater that corresponded to the show's mirror set.

From its first day, *A Chorus Line* had been different. It had started life as a "workshop," a new expression in those times, its staging improvised even while the show was as yet unwritten and uncomposed. It was 1974, the era of encounter groups. Director-choreographer Michael Bennett began by sitting down with a group of Broadway gypsies and encouraging them to talk about dancing, how they got interested in it as children and what kind of adult lives it gave them. Forty hours of taped conversations later, he began to put the show together, the first musical to be created on its feet, and in that it was not merely different from other musicals; more important, it was entirely different from plays, a creature purely of the theater, born and raised there, its staging the "writing." No longer related to conventional drama in any way — no longer remotely a musical play — the Broadway musical had finally assumed an identity that was completely its own.

Aptly enough, this was a musical about musicals, an artistic musical about commercial musicals, and destined to be the ultimate Broadway musical, the "There's No Business Like Show Business" of musicals.

At the end of every performance, as the years began to pass, no audience could resist the crowning conclusion, an archetypal Broadway finale, a chorus line high-kicking its way into eternity. Tourists and Broadway toughies alike were thrilled by that finale, and even those inured to hokum and quick to scoff at sentiment would applaud and weep. Even as the dancers in that culminating chorus line were building to a climax beyond decency, dipping in their gold satin costumes, even still the applause would continue as underscoring. And the applause would turn back upon itself, the audience applauding for itself and for show business and for the wonderful luck to be in or at least near it, foolish and dopey as it was.

And the metaphor of it? What did it mean? Humanity (as Bennett claimed)? Is that what the applause and the tears were for? No. Better. The applause and tears were for glitzy finales, for outrageous and ridiculous, *reckless* joy in a darkened theater.

"No show runs forever," Bennett said on his deathbed in 1987, but to run forever was the meaning of his high-kicking finale. Glitz eternal. After two hours and ten minutes of classic steps, drill and rehearsal, rejection and hope, this conclusive line of high-kicking dancers was the only possibility for a closing number. Bennett had achieved the essential quality of a classic: inevitability.

The triumph of *A Chorus Line* lay in its ability to thrill most people; its greatness lay in the artistry that was necessary to achieve that thrill. But in the commercial theater, there cannot be a *succès d'estime*. There can perhaps be a prestigious flop. A show can get fancy reviews and not draw an audience and close early and win a prize. Or a show can win a prize and run a year and lose every cent. But on Broadway, such shows are not successes, of esteem or anything else. They are flops. That is why, in the commercial theater, a show can't be really great unless it succeeds not only by artistic standards but by commercial ones as well, like *Guys and Dolls, My Fair Lady,* or *Fiddler on the Roof.* Audiences must not only stamp their feet but storm the box office to pay for the privilege, and that is why *A Chorus Line* was the culminating Broadway musical.

There were rumors toward the end about returning it to Joseph Papp's Public Theater, where it had started but, as Papp said perfectly, "Why step back? It's the symbol of Broadway."

The *symbol of Broadway* was the musical of gritty hoofers, of greasepaint dancers in tights and leg warmers. It was celebrating not the stars but the company, not Carol Channing or Angela Lansbury but the dancers backing them up as they sang. That is what "One" — the number being rehearsed in *A Chorus Line* — is all about, the star turn without the star. It is about, well, the chorus, and as the show played out the last of its performances, the tears for those dancers flowed anew, and they were good, cheap show business tears, not for pain or tragedy but for the baloney of *the business.* They were harmless sequin tears for the thumping hoofers and the rising trumpets, the dancers edging out of the upstage darkness and toward the audience — a standard ploy to thrill an audience. "I can give them a rush whenever I want to," the show-wise Bennett once boasted, and he was making good on the boast.

The announcement of the final performance boosted business, as closing announcements usually do, and why should *A Chorus Line* have been different in that respect? After a four-week extension it finally shut the doors on April 28, 1990.

There will of course always be revivals but there will never again be the same original production running in the same original Shubert Theatre across the street from Sardi's restaurant. Running, everyone thought, forever.

The late James Coco, a
darling performer, takes
center stage in the revival
of *Little Me*. The show's
brilliant lyricist, Carolyn
Leigh, died in 1983.

Michael Bennett's *Ballroom*
was overcome by the
burden of comparisons
following his *A Chorus Line*.
Vincent Gardenia and
Dorothy Loudon were the
middle-aged lovers in
Ballroom.

The delightful George Rose *(center)* was as comfortable in such flops as *Dance a Little Closer* as he was in such successful musicals as *My Fair Lady, The Pirates of Penzance,* and *The Mystery of Edwin Drood.* He died the victim of a bizarre murder in the Dominican Republic.

if they were animated. Other than these unusual decorative elements, the only other major piece of scenic lumber was an enormous horizontal beam that was raised and lowered from the flies above by cables.

With these striking visual qualities and continuity of music and movement, *Dreamgirls* developed a rhythm, a momentum, a choreographic intensity that made it dynamic. Many of the staging ideas that Michael Bennett conceived for this show, and for *A Chorus Line,* and for *Follies* even earlier, would be extended, a decade later, by Tommy Tune in his production of *Grand Hotel.*

Although *Dreamgirls* was well received, Bennett felt that it was not yet finished, and a year later he was still tinkering with it. By the third year on Broadway, *Dreamgirls* was complete, and it was a masterwork.

As co-producer of *A Chorus Line* as well as its director and choreographer, by 1981 he was unimaginably wealthy. The show was still a worldwide bonanza, but he was a fellow with few material interests. He bought a pair of white Rolls-Royces, one for each coast, but the truth was that he didn't care about cars or about much else besides musicals. (He even decided against directing movies.) And so he bought a Manhattan building and renovated it into the best rehearsal space in New York. There he began work on a new show in collaboration with the popular songwriter Jimmy Webb ("By the Time I Get to Phoenix," "Up, Up and Away"). The show was called *Scandals* and its workshop became the hot rumor along Broadway, but after a year's work, Bennett decided against it. And that was when Bernard B. Jacobs, president of the Shubert Organization (which owns most of New York's theaters) brought him a recording of the British rock opera *Chess*.

When Bennett agreed to stage it, he seemed to move even closer to merging the two significant developments in modern musical theater, concept musicals and through-composed shows. *Chess*, in fact, was written by Andrew Lloyd Webber's former partner Tim Rice, and the music was by Benny Andersson and Bjorn Ulvaeus of the Swedish rock group ABBA.

Like *Evita* and *Cats* earlier, *Chess* was a popular success as a recording before any production of it began. One of the songs, "One Night in Bangkok," was already climbing to the top of the European pop charts.

Jacobs suggested an Anglo-American production originating in London, perhaps to garner the same kind of anticipatory enthusiasm that had given *Evita* and *Cats* such huge advance ticket sales on Broadway. Bennett flew to London to cast the show, supervise script revisions, and work with designer Robin Wagner on the scenic concept. It was the era of spectaculars following in the wake of *Cats*, and now there were *Starlight Express* and *Les Misérables* in addition to imitative, less successful all-sung musicals in London. *Chess*, too, was going to be an extravaganza, its stage dominated by twin chessboards made of television monitors.

But with rehearsals beginning, and with the sets being built, and with a burgeoning advance sale at the London box office, Bennett became too ill to continue. He began a desperate search for medical help, dragging himself across Europe and the breadth of America, but despite his *Chorus Line* fortune, he had no more hope than a penniless victim of AIDS and he died of it at the age of forty-four in July 1987.

Of all the losses to the musical theater, the most striking, because the most symbolic, were the deaths of the two women who meant Broadway at its most thrilling and most innocent: Ethel Merman and Mary Martin. In recognizing them, appreciating and loving and understanding who they were and what they represented, we can grasp the reason why musicals became so popular, why they have changed, and why they will endure.

Merman and Martin were everything that the theater was before television, rock-and-roll, blockbuster movies, and laptop computers. Their product was themselves. They were the show, alone, out of the dark, in the spotlight, in the fantasy. Bold and dauntless, they would open their arms and fling themselves into the audience, to grin and sing as if their charm and nerve could protect them from rejection. Small wonder audiences cared for, looked after, and doted on these stars.

And in those days, audiences applauded the performer rather than the scenery.

Ethel Merman was a force of nature. When she strode on stage it seemed as if she didn't care (or perhaps even know) what the show was, who her character was, who else was on stage, or what the story was about. Even her singing was physical. "It's not just a voice," Cole Porter said. "She's like another instrument in the band."

In later times, ambitions for musical theater were such that the excitement around a mere performer was not justification enough to create a hit show. Both

One of the conflicts between Tim Rice and Andrew Lloyd Webber was Rice's preference for rock music over theatrical. When the lyricist collaborated on *Chess* with two musicians from the group ABBA, he got the kind of hit song he longed for, "One Night in Bangkok."

Stephen Sondheim and Arthur Laurents resented Merman's self-indulgence, her lack of subtlety, and her carelessness in their *Gypsy* (a show in which she was merely unforgettable). But there was no avoiding Merman if she happened to be on a stage, no greater chance than of avoiding a hurricane. She simply planted her feet at center, reared back, and blasted off. If she seemed loud, vulgar, hopelessly and foolishly old-fashioned, there was still no getting out of her way. There is no such human force today. Time, taste, and amplification have swept all that into the past.

Mary Martin was, contrastingly, coy. Her stage tricks were subtle in comparison to the Merman bravado, although by contemporary standards, she too would be considered a shameless thespian. Demure as Martin might have seemed, sunny and radiant and almost brainlessly cheerful, she was also a theatrical magnet, and when she was on stage, anything else was hard to notice. One way or another, Mary Martin made certain of that.

As time passed and as they grew older, some of their roles seemed ill-suited and even embarrassing. Merman hardly cut a romantic figure playing Annie Oakley at the age of 57 in a 1966 revival of *Annie Get Your Gun*. Martin was slightly mature, at 46, to be playing a novitiate in *The Sound of Music*. But allowances were made in those days as they are not in these because the musical theater still had one foot planted on a footlit stage where greasepaint and paper moons were the rule.

Ours is a smarter and more sophisticated stage world. Our musicals are better crafted, there is no doubt of it.

Alas, what we have lost.

Bob Fosse's distinctive dance movement characterized *Big Deal*.

Overleaf:
A final look at another moment in the brilliant George Ballanchine choreography for the *On Your Toes* revival of 1983.

213

In a brilliant stage effect for
Dreamgirls, Bennett
reversed the audience's
point of view.

ACKNOWLEDGMENTS

The help of many people was necessary to the writing of this book and I am grateful to them for providing it so graciously. Andrew Lloyd Webber, Harold Prince, Tommy Tune, and Cameron Mackintosh were free with their conversational time. Tony Walton was generous with photos of his model sets, Santo Loquasto with costume sketches, and Henry Grossman with photographs of the *Grand Hotel* workshop. As ever, the staff at the Theatre Collection of The New York Public Library at Lincoln Center was always at hand with the appropriate reference and the correct call numbers. Broadway's press agents, the unsung working enthusiasts of the professional theater, were amiably available for identifying the actors in the photographs. The photographs, of course, are essential to this book and I'm glad that John Crowley was my picture editor again, to pursue them so relentlessly and successfully. Carey Lovelace copyedited the text with a rare combination of toughness and compliments, the former necessary for quality, the latter for ego. Luckily for me, Peter Simon's proofreading kept my facts straight. Most of the wonderful photographs were taken by a wonderful photographer, Martha Swope, who has become the visual chronicler of Broadway. She is not only a colleague on this book but a friend and advisor. The book in itself is a beautiful thing thanks to Warren Infield, who has designed every page of it. Perhaps most important, the choice harmony of word, thought, illustration, and sensibility has been struck, protected, and maintained by my friend and editor, Bob Morton. In a world where even writers create on television screens, he remembers the importance of words and ideas, and the joy of making a book.

INDEX

Page numbers in *italics* indicate illustrations.

Broadway has yet to prove itself so cynically commercial that it can support sequels. *Annie II* involved the same team of authors as the beloved original. Even Dorothy Loudon was back as the evil Miss Hannigan. The show's Washington tryout was so calamitous that the out-of-town closing made front page news in New York.

Oh, Brother was pure flop. The notion — a musical version of Shakespeare's *A Comedy of Errors* — had not only been done before (as *The Boys From Syracuse*) but in this version was beyond ludicrous. *Oh, Brother* switched Shakespeare to the contemporary Middle East. The Ayatollah was one of its characters. The show closed the day after it opened in 1981, bringing down with it some very agreeable music by composer Michael Valente.

Some performers are doomed by prejudice, and their vehicles sink with them. A 1982 revival of George M. Cohan's *Little Johnny Jones*, was not without its charms. One of them was television star Donny Osmond, but his image was of a kiddie act. The show closed on opening night.

There is no recipe for failure so reliable as the mixing of Broadway musicals and the inexperienced. *Marilyn*, a very expensive learning experience, ran for two weeks in 1983.

Rags was a failure only in Broadway's cruelest sense: it closed quickly (after two performances in 1986) and lost everything. It nevertheless was not a waste of time or talent. This musical about the Jewish immigrant experience had majestic ambitions, beginning with a Charles Strouse score that attempted (and regularly achieved) a striking blend of ragtime, Yiddish klezmer music, and Strouse's own musicianly lyricism. The lyrics were by Stephen Schwartz and the libretto by Joseph Stein — both proven professionals. The electrifying soprano Teresa Stratas headed the cast. The elements were impeccable but the combination did not work.

Captions for the overture section in the front of the book.

Page 1: Broadway itself was one of the subjects of *The Tap Dance Kid.*

Pages 2–3: A massive lifting, rotating erector set for *Starlight Express* made it the ultimate show about scenery.

Pages 4–5: Director–choreographer Bob Fosse staged the marvelous Cy Coleman–Dorothy Fields song "Big Spender" with such originality and style that audiences took it as a dance number. The number ultimately became a Broadway classic.

Page 6: Andrew Lloyd Webber's "The Music of the Night" was set in the breathtaking underground lagoon of *The Phantom of the Opera.*

Pages 10–11: Before and after: the female impersonators of *La Cage aux Folles* reveal themselves near the show's ending.

PHOTO CREDITS

© Clive Barda/London: 6, 68, 70, 74, 76–77; © Alan J. Berliner: 27; © Donald Cooper/Photostage: 58, 126, 128, 130, 131, 135, 136, 138; © Peter Cunningham: 16, 67, 69, 71, 132–33, 143, 171, 173, 197 right, 210; © Kenn Duncan: 25, 73, 100–101; © Henry Grossman: 110, 111 left; © Beatrice Heyligers: 190; © Brigitte Lacombe: 14–15; © Michael Le Poer Trench: 127, 129, 134, 137; ©Santo Loquasto: 109, 111 right; © Joan Marcus: 176; © Bob Marshak: 191; Museum of the City of New York, Theatre Collection: 198 above; New York Public Library at Lincoln Center, Billy Rose Theatre Collection: 198 below, 199; © Martha Swope: 1, 2–3, 4–5, 9, 10–13, 17–24, 26, 28, 28–29, 30 right, 32–33, 34, 36, 38–42, 45, 46–49, 50–52, 54, 55 below, 57, 59, 60–61, 62–66, 75, 78, 80–85, 87, 89 below, 90–91, 93–94, 96–97, 98, 99, 102–108, 112–16, 118, 119, 121–23, 125, 139–42, 144–46, 149–51, 153, 154, 156–57, 158–63, 164 below, 165 below, 166, 167, 168–69, 170, 172, 174, 175, 178, 179, 180–81, 182–85, 187, 188–89, 192–94, 196–97, 198, 199, 200–201, 202, 203, 204–205, 208, 209, 211–13, 214–15, 216, 219; © Martha Swope, photo Carol Rosegg: 89 above, 164 above, 165 above; © Jay Thompson: 55 above.

Endpaper posters:
Anything Goes © James McMullan, *Aspects of Love* © ™ 1988 R.U.G. PLC "Designed and Printed by DEWYNTERS Ltd."; *Cats*™ © 1981 The Really Useful Group, PLC, designed and printed by DEWYNTERS, Ltd.; *City of Angels* © Serino Coyne, Inc.; *Dreamgirls* © 1981 The Dreams Company; *Evita* © poster produced by kind permission of the Robert Stigwood Organisation and David Land; *42nd Street* designed by Robin Wagner; *Grand Hotel* © Serino Coyne Inc.; *Into the Woods* photo: Peter Cunningham for LeDonne & Wilner, Logo Art: Heidi Landesman; *Les Misérables* "Use of the artwork and logo for *LES MISÉRABLES* is by Permission of Cameron Mackintosh Overseas Limited. © 1985.; *Little Shop of Horrors* designed by DAVID EDWARD BYRD; *Miss Saigon* "Use of the artwork and logo for MISS SAIGON is by permission of Cameron Mackintosh Limited. © 1988."; *The Mystery of Edwin Drood* © Paul Davis; *Nine* © Todd Ruff 1982; *The Phantom of the Opera* LOGO & MASK ™ R.U.G. PLC © 1986 R.U.G. PLC; "Designed and Printed by DEWYNTERS Ltd."; *Starlight Express*™ © The Really Useful Group, PLC, designed and printed by DEWYNTERS Ltd., London; *Sunday in the Park With George* © 1984 Fraver.

SONG CREDITS

"The American Dream"
from MISS SAIGON—a musical by Alain Boublil and Claude-Michel Schönberg
Music by: Claude-Michel Schönberg
Lyrics by: Richard Maltby Jr. and Alain Boublil
© 1987, 1988, 1989, 1990

"The Best of Times" from *La Cage aux Folles*
Music and Lyric by Jerry Herman
© 1983 JERRY HERMAN
All Rights Controlled by JERRYCO MUSIC CO.
Exclusive Agent: EDWIN H. MORRIS & COMPANY, A Division of MPL Communications, Inc. International Copyright Secured
All Rights Reserved

City of Angels Theme
(Cy Coleman)
© 1989, 1990 NOTABLE MUSIC CO., INC.
All rights administered by WB MUSIC CORP.
All rights Reserved. Used by Permission.

Excerpts From *The Phantom of the Opera*
By Andrew Lloyd Webber, Charles Hart, Richard Stilgoe and Mike Batt
Copyright © 1986 by THE REALLY USEFUL GROUP plc.
Used by permission. ALL RIGHTS RESERVED

"Gigolo"
(Cole Porter)
© 1929 WARNER BROS. INC. (Renewed)
All Rights Reserved. Used by Permission.

"Gypsy"
(Stephen Sondheim, Jule Styne)
© 1960 WILLIAMSON MUSIC & STRATFORD MUSIC CORP.
All Rights administered by Chappell & Co.
All Rights Reserved. Used by Permission.

"The Heat is On in Saigon"
from *MISS SAIGON*—a musical by Alain Boublil and Claude-Michel Schönberg
Music by: Claude-Michel Schönberg
Lyrics by: Richard Maltby Jr. and Alain Boublil
© 1987, 1988, 1989, 1990

"I'M STILL HERE" (by Stephen Sondheim)
© Copyright 1971—RANGE ROAD MUSIC INC./QUARTET MUSIC INC./RILTING MUSIC INC./BURTHEN MUSIC COMPANY INC.
Used by permission. All Rights reserved.

"I Am What I Am" from *La Cage aux Folles*
Music and Lyric by Jerry Herman
© 1983 JERRY HERMAN
All Rights Controlled by JERRYCO MUSIC CO.
Exclusive Agent: EDWIN H. MORRIS & COMPANY, A Division of MPL Communications, Inc. International Copyright Secured
All Rights Reserved

"I CAN'T BE BOTHERED NOW"
(George Gershwin, Ira Gershwin)
© 1937 (Renewed) CHAPPEL & CO. (ASCAP)
All Rights Reserved. Used by Permission.

"The Kid Inside"
Words and Music by Craig Carnelia
© Copyright 1983 Carnelia Music
c/o A. Schroeder International Ltd.
International Copyright Secured
Used by permission, all rights reserved

Maltby Rights
© 1984 Fiddleback Music Publishing Co., Inc.
& Progeny Music & Revelation Music Publishing Corp.
& Long Pond Music
All Rights Reserved. Reprinted by special permission.

"Merrily We Roll Along"
© 1981 Revelation Music Publishing Corp. & Rilting Music, Inc.
All Rights Reserved
Reprinted by special permission

"The Movie in My Mind"
from MISS SAIGON—a musical by Alain Boublil and Claude-Michel Schönberg
Music by: Claude-Michel Schönberg
Lyrics by: Richard Maltby Jr. and Alain Boublil
© 1987, 1988, 1989, 1990

"Sunday in the Park with George"
© 1984 Revelation Music Publishing Corp. & Rilting Music, Inc.
All Rights Reserved
Reprinted by special permission

"Sweeney Todd"
© 1978 Revelation Music Publishing Corp. & Rilting Music, Inc.

"Who Couldn't Dance With You?", Words and music by Robert Wright and George Forrest (with Wally Harper). Reprinted by permission of Scheffel Music Corp., New York, New York.